GRASP TIGHT THE OLD WAYS

Selections from the Klamer Family Collection of Inuit Art

Jean Blodgett

Art Gallery of Ontario
Musée des beaux-arts de l'Ontario
Toronto Canada

Canadian Cataloguing in Publication Data

Blodgett, Jean 1945 –
Grasp tight the old ways

Catalogue of an exhibition held at the Art Gallery of Ontario,
May 28 – July 31, 1983
Bibliography: p.
ISBN 0-919876-92-7

1. Inuit – Canada – Prints – Exhibitions.
2. Inuit – Canada – Sculpture – Exhibitions.
3. Prints, Canadian – Exhibitions.
4. Sculpture, Canadian – Exhibitions.
5. Klamer family – Art collections.
I. Art Gallery of Ontario. II. Title.

NE541.4.B46   769.9719'074'0113541   C83-094094-4

Itinerary of the Exhibition

Art Gallery of Ontario, Toronto
May 28 – July 31, 1983

The Winnipeg Art Gallery, Winnipeg
November 10, 1983 – January 2, 1984

Field Museum of Natural History, Chicago
February 27 – May 27, 1984

Glenbow Museum, Calgary
June 20 – August 15, 1984

Art Gallery of Greater Victoria, Victoria
September 13 – October 21, 1984

McCord Museum, Montreal
November 15, 1984 – January 13, 1985

Confederation Centre Art Gallery and Museum, Charlottetown
February 21 – April 7, 1985

The Art Gallery of Ontario is funded by the Province of Ontario,
the Ministry of Citizenship and Culture, the Municipality of
Metropolitan Toronto, and the Government of Canada through the
National Museums Corporation, the Museums Assistance Programmes
of the National Museums of Canada, and the Canada Council.

On the Cover: Aqjangajuk Shaa (1937 –), *Figure with Ulu*, c. 1967;
green stone, 38.5 x 47.0 x 6.0 cm. 78/199
Detail on front cover; complete work on back cover.

CONTENTS

MAP OF INUIT
ART CENTRES

Resol

Tuktoyaktuk

Aklavik ● ●Inuvik

● Holman

Paulatuk

Victoria Island

Cambridge Bay ●

Gjoa Ha

● Coppermine

Northwe

● Yellowknife

Grise Fiord

Greenland

Arctic Bay ● Pond Inlet

Clyde River

Broughton Island

Baffin Island

Pangnirtung

Spence Bay

Igloolik ● Hall Beach

Pelly Bay

Repulse Bay

Frobisher Bay

Cape Dorset ● Lake Harbour

Coral Harbour

Territories

Baker Lake

Kangiqsujuak
(Wakeham Bay)

Ivujivik ● Salluit
(Sugluk)

Kangirsuk
(Payne Bay)

Kangiqsualujjuaq
(George River)

Chesterfield Inlet

Rankin Inlet

Whale Cove

Akulivik

Povungnituk

Kuujjuaq
(Fort Chimo)

Arctic Quebec / Nouveau Québec

Eskimo Point

Inukjuak
(Port Harrison)

Hudson Bay

Sanikiluaq
(Belcher Islands)

Kuujjuaraapik
(Great Whale River)

FOREWORD

In December 1978 the Art Gallery of Ontario accepted, into its Permanent Collection, works of Inuit art that my wife Marcia and I had collected over a period of some years. It was our wish that selections from this collection would be on display at all times and that portions of it would travel. In this way many people, especially the people of Canada, would be able to enjoy the beauty of this work, might become aware of the Inuit's inherent artistic talent, and come to understand that a wondrous Eskimo heritage has existed for thousands of years. While the bulk of our collection is contemporary and from the Canadian Arctic, there are some examples from prehistoric and historic eras, and from different geographic areas, including Alaska. The works cover a time span of some 2000 years.

When we were assembling, choosing, and inventorying works for our gift, we experienced at once the excitement and joy of seeing old friends – that thrill of discovery which is always there when we look at favourite objects – and the sad realization that we would be parting with many of them. We were amazed at the number of objects we had accumulated. Some people may approach their collection in a methodical, organized, and researched way. Such was not the case with us. It was not a particular artist, or place, or type of work that we chose. We were drawn to Inuit art at first for non-intellectual reasons, attracted to it just as we had been to modern art because of its vigour and freshness, and we sensed its deep spiritual quality.

Part of this appeal for me may have been due to my empathy with the north and northern people. It was there that the greater part of my childhood and youth was spent. It was at The Pas, Manitoba (500 miles north of Winnipeg) in the early 1900s that my father began his life in Canada as a merchant fur trader. He travelled by canoe and dog team. I grew up witnessing the plight of the Indian, listening to stories and legends told by these early pioneers. I recall travelling with my father, at the age of six, on a two-day journey by railway gas-car and canoe to a remote settlement under cold, stormy conditions. As a young man I worked in the bush, sleeping in a tent in arctic temperatures. The north was part of my heritage, and I am sure this played a part in the development of my interest in the Eskimo and their art. Fortunately, Marcia had a similar feeling for the art and the people, so we have been able to share many years of satisfying study and collecting.

The Inuit are an amazing people. There is no higher concentration of artists per capita, per settlement than among the Inuit people. From the outset of their contemporary sculpture, printmaking, and textile projects – projects encouraged by white people – it was clear that they are truly gifted artists. The Eskimo people have survived millennia in the hardest physical environment inhabited by man, unaffected by outside influence until recent time. Their survival required the utmost skill, ingenuity, and resourcefulness imaginable. The power of their spiritual world and of the shaman became major forces in their lives, as they strived to keep the universe in balance. They were alone with nature in a land of constant change – what was possible yesterday cannot be done today. Where we would see endless, empty space, the Inuit saw life. Nothing escaped them and their observations were incessant.

Shamanistic objects and symbols, tools and weapons, clothing and functional objects all had to be created from the materials at hand. Because of their design and beauty they truly were art objects, and this esthetic sense touched all aspects of Eskimo life. Many of the same kinds of utilitarian things were made over and over once a design had been perfected. Their concerns, their spiritual world, had been the same century after century. Changes in decorative styles occurred slowly over the centuries for a given group. It is no wonder that their contemporary work reflects so much of the past. One notices an incredible continuity of subject matter, styles, and interest from prehistoric time to the present. Today's work is not only bound by the cultural necessities of the past, it reflects the present by the individual style and personality of the artist with the added dimension of their tradition. There is an honesty and gentleness in their work that reflects an invincible serenity in the face of their harsh environment. The instinct of self-preservation developed a humility and a respect for the power of nature, a togetherness of unspoken harmony, a love of one for the other. There is a majesty, simplicity, and loving quality in whatever they create. Their work radiates a warmth and spirituality that one senses immediately.

I remember attending the first one-man show of Inuit art at the Innuit Gallery in Toronto. Here was Aqjangajuk, a renowned hunter, now artist, on his first visit south. He stood stoically, completely unperturbed, amid the excitement of an opening, clutching a long-stemmed rose all night, as if it was the most precious thing on earth. Here was a man from the barren north, sensitive to the delicacy and beauty of a rose. He had never seen a flower so large.

It was a special thrill to meet Aqjangajuk because his was the first Inuit sculpture we had bought, and the majority of our first pieces were his. We instinctively chose his work, without knowing whose it was; in those years little attention was given to the sculptor's name. He visited us and we were impressed by his dignity, charm, and composure in a completely strange environment. Through his interpreter I enquired if anything had impressed Aqjangajuk on his visit. At first the interpreter shrugged and said "not really"; then her face lit up as she described how animated and excited Aqjangajuk had become when, in a park, he saw a horse running. Apparently he shrieked for joy at the beauty of that moment. No artist can capture the natural movement of an animal better than the Inuit, and many of their sculptures depict such action to perfection.

Several years later, the well-known artists Kenojuak and Kananginak were in Toronto for a special exhibit, and my wife and I invited them to have lunch with us. Kananginak kept turning around and looking out our diningroom window. I finally realized that he wished to go outside, but was too polite to ask; through his interpreter I invited him to do so. He quickly got up from his chair, went outside, dropped to his knees, and began to pick up the leaves that had fallen from a huge maple tree. We wrapped them carefully, as he wished to take them home. For me, these were magical moments because they gave me insight into the sensitive and caring nature of these people.

Our interest in Inuit art began in 1961 when we purchased two 1960 Cape Dorset prints. We were fortunate in our travels away from Canada to find and bring home many beautiful Inuit works, many of which became favourites of ours. We always felt we had been mysteriously guided to these treasures as we discovered them in the most unlikely places. In 1962 on a trip to Europe we happened by chance to visit the Gimpel Gallery in London. Mrs. Gimpel, a former Canadian from Winnipeg, showed us through the gallery where we saw Cape Dorset sculptures, and later, in their home, their private collection of Inuit art. This visit strongly influenced our future direction, since here was an individual – the late Charles Gimpel – a second-generation art dealer from Paris, who flew to Cape Dorset every year to select works for his gallery and his private collection. We saw exquisite objects and realized then that this art was as good as that produced by any culture.

It was not until 1964 in Toronto, however, that we bought our first piece of Inuit sculpture, the Aqjangajuk. In San Francisco in 1969, we saw to our amazement an exciting show of Cape Dorset drawings at the Palace of the Legion of Honor. To our added excitement we were directed to a gallery opening that evening and brought back to Toronto a few early prints and drawings and a majestic Osuitok bear (No. 71), another of our favourites. On a trip to Israel, out walking one evening, we saw Inuit art in a shop window in Tel Aviv. Next morning we went back and found fine works that had been carved in the fifties. Once again we brought important works back to Canada. It was later that I learned that one of the pieces was by Nayoumealook (No. 118), one of the finest carvers of that time.

While on a ski trip to Aspen in the early 1970s, Marcia went browsing in the shops and discovered some Alaskan artifacts. This led to the purchase of our first historic and prehistoric material. We became aware of a completely new area of Eskimo culture and we were fortunate to obtain many fine examples of this period. It enhanced our appreciation for our contemporary pieces because there was such a profound relationship between the old and the new. Again, in Amsterdam in 1976, I happened to glance at a newspaper and recognized an announcement of an Inuit exhibit. We rushed to the gallery and saw a wonderful exhibition – the first ever in Holland. On the flight back our son Joseph carried, with great care, a beautiful large Joanassie Cape Dorset bird (No. 41), another favourite. So, for us, special finds seemed just to happen, and added greatly to our joy in collecting.

We have never collected for collecting's sake. We chose a piece simply because we liked it. It appealed to our esthetic sensibilities and gave us enjoyment. Over the years at home and in our travels we viewed many aspects of art. The more we saw, the more it reinforced for us, the validity and importance of preserving the cultural heritage of what we thought was the best of early and contemporary Inuit art. It was with this realization, in the mid-seventies, that we began to collect more earnestly.

From the moment we bought our first piece of Inuit sculpture we never had any doubt about which pieces we considered best in a given exhibition. Marcia would look at an exhibition without knowing my first choice and invariably pick the same work. So we were fortunate in being able to avoid, from the beginning, conflicts over such decisions. Our children, Marianne and Joseph, were exposed to Inuit art at an early age and learned to appreciate it. Many of the pieces in this collection were bought for them, so this is truly a "family collection." How fortunate and how privileged we have been to share this common interest.

We are truly indebted to the many Eskimo artists past and present who, in creating their art, preserved their heritage for all people to see, study and enjoy. This art deserves world-wide attention. We sincerely thank the Art Gallery of Ontario for producing this major exhibit and arranging for the exhibition to visit other cities. We wish to express our warm appreciation and thanks to William J. Withrow, Director of the Art

Gallery of Ontario, whose guidance and dedicated concern made this possible. To Jean Blodgett, Curator, our thanks for her many hours of work, her expertise and devotion in curating this exhibition and writing this comprehensive catalogue. At all times we have been appreciative of the sensitivity toward and understanding of the collection by everyone involved.

We hope that those who see the exhibition and read this catalogue can capture some of the affection our family feels for this remarkable art.

Harry Klamer

PREFACE

With this book and the exhibition it records, the Art Gallery of Ontario gratefully acknowledges the generous donation of Inuit art works by Mr. and Mrs. Harry Klamer and their family.

The Klamers were first attracted to Inuit art some twenty years ago. Recognizing its qualities, they became enthusiastic patrons, seeking out exhibitions, acquiring pieces, travelling to the north, and championing this art form at home and abroad. Their collecting over the years has been inspired as much by their own personal appreciation as by their belief that the best of this art should be preserved. Their desire to document the accomplishments of Inuit artists and to make these works of art available for others to see led them to donate a portion of their collection to the Art Gallery of Ontario in 1978.

Since then, in keeping with the Klamers' desire to share their collection with others, pieces have been shown in a number of ongoing displays at the Gallery and in an exhibition organized for the University of Guelph in 1980.

Also during this time preparations have been underway for the exhibition that this book documents. The collection of more than 600 carvings, drawings, prints, and wall hangings has been catalogued and researched by Curator Jean Blodgett, who also has had the difficult task of narrowing down a selection of works for the exhibition. Those pieces are all illustrated here with accompanying texts, and we would like to take this opportunity to thank Ms. Blodgett for her capable and thorough work, and to express our appreciation to Dorothy Jean Ray, Henry B. Collins, and James W. VanStone for their contributions to this book.

Exhibitions of this nature call for concerted and long-term efforts on the part of the members of the staff at the Gallery; to them our sincere thanks and a special tribute.

We are particularly glad that the exhibition will be travelling to various centres in Canada and to the Field Museum in Chicago, where others will have the opportunity to enjoy this fine collection. Funds from the Canada Council and the National Museums of Canada have enabled us to organize and tour the Klamer Collection exhibition, and their assistance is gratefully acknowledged.

Over the years the Art Gallery of Ontario has sponsored and hosted other exhibitions of Inuit art, but this is the first time that a major exhibition has been organized from the Gallery's own permanent Inuit collection. This exhibition, then, is offered with pride, and with gratitude to the Klamer family and the many artists originally responsible for creating the works.

William J. Withrow,
Director, Art Gallery of Ontario

ACKNOWLEDGEMENTS

Comparative analysis of the individual artist's work in this exhibition would not have been possible without the resources of the Inuit Art Section of the Department of Indian Affairs and Northern Development and the Canadian Ethnology Service of the National Museum of Man. For their assistance and access to their biography files, resource material, slides and photographs, my heartfelt thanks to Deborah Smith, Daniela Planka and the other staff members of the Inuit Art Section, and to Odette Leroux, Curator of Inuit Art, National Museum of Man.

Other individuals who helped with the research for this exhibition and provided valuable information are Mary Craig, La Fédération des Coopératives du Nouveau Québec; Dave Sutherland, Arts and Crafts Development Officer, Government of the Northwest Territories; Bernadette Driscoll and Fabiola Bohemier, Winnipeg Art Gallery; Darlene Wight, Canadian Arctic Producers Ltd. I would also like to thank Norman Hallendy for letting me read his essay on Kiakshuk.

To those who answered my many queries in and about particular communities I am deeply indebted: Ruby Angrna'naaq, Sheila Butler, and John Pudnak, Baker Lake; Wallace Brannen, Patricia and Terrence Ryan, Cape Dorset; David Alagalak, Eskimo Point; Ann Hanson, Frobisher Bay; Fred Weihs, Lake Harbour; Jean Burke, Pelly Bay; Mike Kenny and Glenn LeClair, Rankin Inlet; Elroy Anderson, Repulse Bay.

Grateful acknowledgement is also made for the Inuktitut translations included here: John Houston acted as interpreter in my interview with Kenojuak, John Pudnak translated the text on the Janet Kigusiuq drawing, Mukshowya Niviaqsi the text on the Pitseolak drawing, and Maudie Qitsualik the phrase on the base of the Aupilarjuk sculpture.

Cataloguing and researching the older artifacts in the Klamer Collection were undertaken with the assistance of several outside experts and I would like to express my gratitude to them all. Dr. Robert McGhee of the Archaeological Survey, National Museum of Man, Ottawa and George Swinton of Carleton University made initial classifications, Saradell Ard Frederick of the University of Alaska, Anchorage helped with further identification, and the final cataloguing was directed by James W. VanStone of the Field Museum of Natural History in Chicago. Dr. VanStone also made suggestions about the artifacts to be included in the exhibition, and has written catalogue entries for several of them. Dorothy Jean Ray, an authority on Alaskan art, and Dr. Henry B. Collins, Archaeologist Emeritus, National Museum of Natural History, Smithsonian Institution, working from photographs, have written catalogue entries for the other Alaskan artifacts included here.

The role of the staff of the Art Gallery of Ontario in the preparation of this catalogue, the exhibition and its tour is gratefully recognized. I would like to pay special tribute to Denise Bukowski, Faye Craig, Grace Desa, Ivan Holmes, Claudette Kernaghan, Cheryl-Anne Luck, Glenda Milrod, Larry Ostrom, John Ruseckas and his staff, Barry Simpson, Ches Taylor, Catherine Van Baren and Kathy Wladyka. To Marie Fleming, who acted as my gallery liason and adviser, my sincere thanks. William Withrow's continued interest and support is also greatly appreciated.

For reading the completed text and making comments and suggestions, I am particularly grateful to Marybelle Myers. Her advice and feedback as well as that of my husband Max Dean have been a great help to me.

Finally, warm thanks to Marcia and Harry Klamer for their cooperation and enthusiasm throughout this project.

INTRODUCTION

One of the discoveries made in the process of cataloguing the Klamer Collection was the Repulse Bay sculpture by Aupilarjuk (No. 150) whose title (taken from the text incised onto the sculpture's base) – *Grasp Tight the Old Ways* – has also been used as the title for this book and exhibition. While many other Inuit artists continue to show traditional scenes and activities in their work, few use their art for such direct statements as Aupilarjuk has made in the Inuktitut phrase incised on his sculpture; a sculpture destined, as he knew, not to be seen by his fellow Inuit, but to be sold in the south (as northerners call all areas south of the Arctic), where only a few could translate his written text. Perhaps his message is, in fact, addressed to us; perhaps it was a sentiment he wished to record regardless of the audience.

While not as outspoken as Aupilarjuk, preserving and documenting the old ways is often the aim of the many artists who continue to portray traditional subjects in their work; work that ignores the tremendous changes taking place in the north at the present time. Although this clinging to the old has been criticized by some as catering to the tastes of the southern market, it is, in many cases, more a reflection of the needs and sentiments of the Inuit artists themselves.

On the one hand the art works are nostalgic yearnings, a remembering and reliving of the past, which as Pitseolak says was a good life (Eber, *Pitseolak: Pictures Out of My Life*, unpaged):

> This was the old Eskimo way of life; you couldn't give up because it was the only way. Today I like living in a house that is always warm but, sometimes, I want to move and go to the camps where I have been. The old life was a hard life but it was good. It was happy.

On the other hand, the art works are a means of recording Inuit lifestyle – both for the Inuit themselves and for their southern customers. That this impetus for artmaking is not better known is perhaps attributable to a basic dearth of information and the fact that most artists – unlike Aupilarjuk – do not make this obvious in their actual work. In their written statements, though, artists may point out the importance of the art as a means of keeping hold of the old ways. Kananginak, quoted later in a discussion of his work (p. 88-89), speaks of the value of carvings and prints for telling of the past, and keeping traditions for the future. Paulosie Kasadluak of Inukjuak in a 1976 essay (The Winnipeg Art Gallery, *Port Harrison/Inoucdjouac*, p. 21) wrote:

> It is not only to make money that we carve. Nor do we carve make-believe things. What we show in our carvings is the life we have lived in the past right up to today. We show the truth.

Considering these sentiments on the part of the Inuit artists themselves and the Klamers' own interest in the Inuit people and their culture, it seemed only appropriate to acknowledge Aupilarjuk's plea by making it the title of the exhibition and book. This is not to say that the Klamers' collecting was inspired and directed solely by a desire to document the traditions of the Inuit. As they have said, they bought pieces because they liked them, and while this criterion has resulted in a collection characterized by expressive and visual qualities, there are also many narrative works that record the traditional culture of these artists the Klamers so admire.

The majority of pieces in the Klamer Collection are contemporary Canadian, including prints, drawings, wall hangings, and sculptures from some twenty communities. About half of these contemporary works are from Cape Dorset. This emphasis on Cape Dorset has resulted in a collection of over 200 prints dating from each yearly collection between 1960 and 1977, as well as some outstanding examples of Cape Dorset sculpture and over forty original drawings. Inuit drawings, unlike the prints, have never been as accessible or as sought after as the prints by most collectors, making the fifty Cape Dorset and Baker Lake drawings in the Klamer Collection a particularly valuable resource.

Among these drawings was another exciting discovery – Lucy's drawing for the print *Family of Birds* (No. 66). Drawings that have been used in the making of prints – being of special interest – are usually retained by the respective cooperatives either as part of their own archives or as a body of work to be housed in a public institution. In this case the Lucy print-drawing, with another title written on the back of the piece of paper, changed hands several times without anyone realizing it was the drawing for a print. It was only in the process of cataloguing that this early drawing was identified as the original for the 1963 print.

In addition to those from Cape Dorset in the collection, there are prints from Baker Lake, Povungnituk, and Holman Island. Again of special interest are the five 1961 graphics from Povungnituk, dating from the first experiments in printmaking there. This group of prints was not catalogued, or even fully documented. A list compiled of the 1961 works by La Fédération des Coopératives du Nouveau-Québec records twenty-one prints, but additional works, including several of the Klamer prints, have continued to come to light over the years. To help document these early experiments, all five 1961 Povungnituk prints are reproduced here.

Two of the Povungnituk prints are made from fibreglass plates cast in wax, an experimental process that was discontinued. Of the printing processes now used in the north, examples of engraving, stonecut, and stencil are included here. Some of the early Cape Dorset prints are described on the print as sealskin stencil. These graphics have been described here simply as stencils since sealskin stencils were used for some experimental proofing but not for the printing of editioned prints.

In the following discussions of printmaking and other art forms in Baker Lake and Cape Dorset, reference is made to several of the non-Inuit people involved and a short description of them is included here. In 1948, James Houston travelled north to the east coast of Hudson Bay; his enthusiasm for the carvings he found there and the examples he brought back with him sparked the beginning of what is now called the contemporary period, which has seen a tremendous increase in interest in and production of Inuit art. In 1951, Houston and his wife Alma travelled to Cape Dorset; there, they encouraged the making of both traditional and new art forms, including printmaking. Terrence Ryan came to Cape Dorset in 1960 and has remained ever since; first acting as arts advisor, he is now the general manager of the West Baffin Eskimo Cooperative. In Baker Lake, Jack and Sheila Butler, who came to the community in 1969, not only helped set up a successful printmaking program, but were supportive of other artistic endeavours and forms of expression, such as sewing.

The printmaking procedures and processes vary somewhat from community to community. The early Povungnituk prints were made from stones cut by the artist whose name appears on the work. With the exception of works by Leah Qumaluk, who also did her own printing, the stones were then printed by (women) printers whose names did not appear on the prints until the late 1970s. In Baker Lake and Cape Dorset, with only a few exceptions when the artist is both originator and printer, the printing is done by the printshop staff using drawings made by the artist or engraved plates cut by them. The stonecut and stencil printing process of tracing the drawing, cutting the stone block and/or stencil, and then inking and printing may involve two or more people. On Baker Lake prints the names of the printers appear written on the print after the name of the artist. On Cape Dorset prints, the printer (only one is recognized even if more were involved in the cutting and printing process) is indicated by a specially designed stamp, or chop, comprised of the syllabics of his name, which appears in one of the corners of the print (along with other chops for the Co-op and the artist). The printer's name does not appear on Cape Dorset engravings.

While the selection of sculpture from Cape Dorset in the collection reflects the Klamers' feeling for the expressive and impressive qualities of work from this community, there are also representative examples from many other settlements; these include intimate folk art scenes from Repulse Bay, representational narrative carvings from Inukjuak, monumental works from Baker Lake, and minimal ones from Rankin Inlet.

In selecting works for the exhibition I have tried to maintain a sampling of pieces that gives an indication of the scope of the Klamer Collection, and while this includes a number of well-known works, especially prints, I have also purposely chosen other works because they were little known and unpublished, or because they shed additional light on an artist's *oeuvre*.

Working with these criteria rather than a single curatorial theme or concept, and making selections from a body of work already preselected, so to speak, by the original collectors, I did not feel that a general essay was a suitable or comprehensive enough means of writing about the various art works. Therefore, each piece, or each artist if there are several works by an individual, is discussed in a separate entry. This approach may not be as successful for comparative analysis but it does allow for more in-depth discussion of each artist or each work.

In writing about the pieces I have been primarily concerned with the individual artist, with how the pieces included here fit into his work, and only secondarily with how they relate to other work from his community and within the broader context of Inuit art in general. I have also tried to make observations and comments that would help the viewer actually look at the piece; to gain a better understanding of the subject matter and the formal concerns.

Writing this type of entry for Inuit art has posed its own kinds of problems. While other art historians who are writing about well-known Western artists would have trouble narrowing down their information, I have had trouble finding even the merest details about some of the artists included here. Aside from the problem of sheer numbers – hundreds of Inuit have made carvings, maybe only one piece in a lifetime – there is a dearth of published information on the individual artists and their work. This lack of data has obviously had a great effect on the content of the entries here. For some artists I simply could find no information beyond basic dates and spelling of names. Even these were sometimes difficult to confirm.

Of Inuit art, the prints are by far the best documented, except for those prints like the 1961 Povungnituk ones. Generally the yearly collections from the printmaking communities are accompanied by a catalogue in which prints are reproduced, often along with other factual and biographical information. Also of great help to me in my work was the comprehensive collection of slides of Inuit prints available in the resource centre at the Inuit Art Section of the Department of Indian Affairs and Northern Development.

Researching the carvings, however, was another matter. Additional examples of the artist's work were found by searching through publications, especially exhibition catalogues, and through the biographical files at Indian and Northern Affairs, and the National Museum of Man. Sometimes I found a number of examples of an artist's work, other times only one reproduction, such as on an invitation for a show, and sometimes no examples at all. Having done all this detective work I have tried to utilize the additional illustrations in the text here, either by referring to the publication if it is accessible, or by reproducing the work as an accompanying figure if I felt it was particularly relevant or pertinent to the discussion.

Not only is there a disappointingly small amount of information on Inuit art, there also remain conflicting and incomplete data. In trying to confirm attributions or obtain further information, I have also directly approached certain communities and artists. Some of the information here is the result of personal interviews in the north and innumerable telephone calls, or interviews undertaken on my behalf by people travelling to or resident in the north. Considering that it can take months to track down the date an artist died, it is perhaps to be expected that second-hand interviewing of this nature is not always productive. And while I was pleasantly surprised by some of the results, I was not surprised by those instances when no information was forthcoming. Those interviewing Inuit artists must contend with cultural differences, language barriers, and reluctance or inability to talk about one's work. While artists everywhere may be unable to verbalize about their work, Inuit artists may simply not wish to discuss certain subjects such as shamanism. In such instances, I have discussed the art works without any mention of what the artist's own interpretation might be, rather than going through the process of naming those who prefer to speak only through their art.

Speaking to us through their carving, graphics, and sewings is certainly something the Inuit artists do most successfully. And while the accompanying discussions here are meant to help the reader understand the work as much as to document the individual artists, these art works are delightfully expressive and informative on their own.

EXPLANATORY NOTES ON THE ENTRIES

Artists are listed alphabetically by surname within communities, with the exception of Cape Dorset, where artists are better known by what we would consider to be their first name.

The sex of the artist is noted with an *m* or *f*, since many Inuit names do not indicate this.

Locations given for the artists are not necessarily their birthplace, but the community they have come to be associated with.

Titles for sculptures, drawings, and wall hangings have been assigned by the curator.

All measurements are in centimetres in the following order: height, width, depth.

Signatures are noted for sculptures, drawings, and wall hangings. These may be in syllabics, Roman, or both. Some artists sign their work solely or additionally with their disc number. The practice of giving a number to each Inuk, which began in the 1940s, has since been discontinued, but older pieces especially are often signed this way.

Reference is, in some cases, made to prints by year and number; 1971/33 is print number 33 in the 1971 print catalogue of the community referred to.

Entries written on the artifacts (Nos. 164-174) are signed with the author's initials: Henry B. Collins (H.B.C.), Dorothy Jean Ray (D.J.R.), James W. VanStone (J.W.VS.).

Throughout this book the term Inuit applies to the present-day Eskimo people of Canada; earlier Canadian cultures and those of other countries, such as Alaska, are referred to as Eskimo.

16.
William Noah (1943-) m.
and Martha Noah (1943-) f.
Baker Lake
Qiviuq's Journey 1973
Stonecut and stencil 6/50
64.0 x 94.0 cm
78/531

21.
Jessie Oonark (1906-) f.
Printed by Simon Tookoome (1934-) m.
Baker Lake
Big Woman 1974
Stonecut and stencil 27/50
62.8 x 94.4 cm
78/167

72. Osuitok Ipeelee (1923-) m.
Cape Dorset
Caribou Head c. 1970
Green stone and antler
54.7 x 31.5 x 45.6 cm
Signed with syllabics
78/244

19

19

59.
Kingmeata (1915-) f.
Cape Dorset
Six Birds c. 1969
Felt-tip pen and graphite
50.7 x 66.5 cm
Signed lower right with syllabics
78/547

25.
Simon Tookoome (1934-) m.
Baker Lake
The Pleasures of Eating Fish 1970
Stonecut and stencil 25/50
64.3 x 94.5 cm
78/650

113.
Nuveeya Ipellie (1920-) m.
Frobisher Bay
Sea Goddess 1976
Dark green stone, ivory, and baleen
22.5 x 26.0 x 10.9 cm
Signed with Roman and dated
78/664

155.
Alexina Panana Naktar (1943-) f.
Repulse Bay
Mother and Child c. 1970
Whalebone, antler, and graphite
22.5 x 10.8 x 9.7 cm
Unsigned
78/202

68.
Lucy (1915-1982) f.
Cape Dorset
Scene 1977
Coloured pencil and acrylic
56.0 x 75.8 cm
Signed lower right with syllabics; dated
   on verso by Cooperative
78/669

110.
Susan Ootnooyuk (1918- c.1975) f.
Eskimo Point
Mother Wearing Necklace and Earrings
   c. 1970
Grey stone, caribou teeth, beads, and sinew
22.0 x 7.6 x 6.3 cm
Signed with syllabics
78/724

52.
Kenojuak (1927-) f.
Cape Dorset
Bird with Colourful Plumage 1970
Felt-tip pen
50.7 x 66.3 cm
Signed lower right with syllabics; dated
on verso by Cooperative
78/176

137.
Joe Talirunili (1899-1976) m.
Povungnituk
Migration c. 1976
Grey stone, wood, hide, and string
29.0 x 18.0 x 31.0 cm
Unsigned
78/185

116.
Elijassiapik (1912-1972) m.
Inukjuak
Mother and Child with Kudlik 1950s
Dark green stone, ivory, light green stone,
   black stone, bone, and blacking
14.0 X 21.5 X 24.7 cm
Signed with syllabics and disc number
78/433

28.
Marion Tuu'luq (1910-   ) f.
Baker Lake
Sun Woman 1975
Wool, felt, embroidery floss and thread
127.0 x 183.0 cm
Signed lower centre with syllabics
78/670

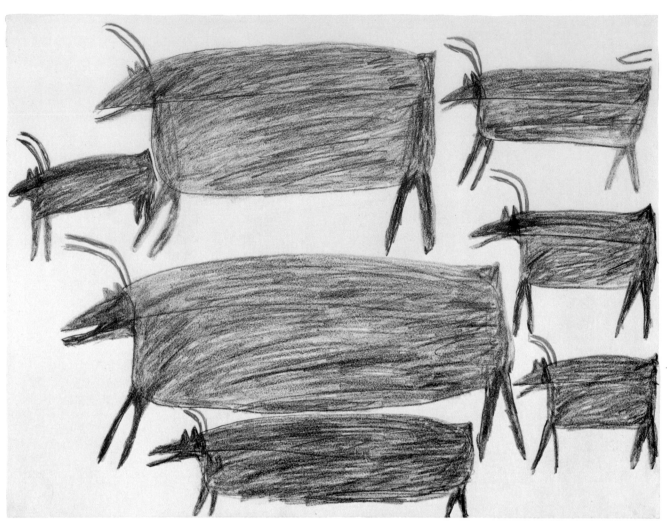

78.
Parr (1893-1969) m.
Cape Dorset
Seven Caribou 1964
Wax crayon
50.8 x 65.8 cm
Signed upper right with syllabics; dated on
verso by Cooperative
78/551

168.
Fat Scraper
Old Bering Sea culture
Bering Strait, Alaska
Ivory
17.0 cm (height)
78/616

121.
Shorty Killiktee (1949-) m.
Lake Harbour
Spirit with Young c. 1969
Green stone and ivory
24.5 x 14.3 x 14.4 cm
Signed with Roman and disc number
78/686

JOSEPH ANGAKTAARYUAQ

In these two sculptures (Nos. 1 and 2) Angaktaaryuaq addresses the subject of the Inuit mother and her child, a theme popular with both male and female carvers, and a ubiquitous image in the north, even today when women continue to carry their babies with them in their parkas. The parka or *amautiq*, with its back pouch or *amaut* for the child, is one of the few pieces of traditional clothing (the other is the *kamik* or boot) that remains in regular use in contemporary times. It is still more appropriate and better suited to Inuit lifestyle and modes of transportation, as well as northern temperatures and geographical terrain, than Snugglies, carriages, or strollers.

Sculptures showing the child simply as an extension of the mother's body, such as a lump on her back, not only represent the child in the *amautiq* but also symbolize the relationship between the two: the dependence of the child on the mother and their continual physical closeness while the child is carried daily by the mother and, at least traditionally, sleeps by her at night. Angaktaaryuaq has conveyed this relationship in both sculptures; one with the baby in the *amautiq*, the other showing the child held in the mother's arms at the front of her body. Here the child's body, faintly indicated by a slight elevation and shallow incised lines, merges into that of the mother, whose broad and enveloping body is articulated only in the facial area.

Such basic treatment of his sculptural subjects is typical of Angaktaaryuaq. Often his figural subjects are only slightly rounded and defined; their prominent feature, the face, is regularly defined with horizontal depressions for eyes and mouth and a ridged vertical nose dished at the sides to suggest the modelling of cheeks. Of the two *Mother and Child* sculptures illustrated here, No. 1 is more elaborately defined, with some indication of hair lines on the top of the mother's head, the hollowing out of space between her legs, and the modelling of the arms – little brackets that extend out and away from the main body.

Angaktaaryuaq was born in the Kazan River area near Baker Lake and was married in that settlement in 1961, but he also lived in Rankin Inlet. While there in the mid-sixties, he began working in clay under Claude Grenier who had started a pottery project in Rankin in the early 1960s. The nickel mine in Rankin Inlet had just closed at the time, leaving residents of the community – a number of whom had moved there because of the jobs at the mine – without employment. Many of the people, presumably Angaktaaryuaq among them, turned to pottery and carving as a source of livelihood. In fact, Angaktaaryuaq's later carving style in works done after he moved back to Baker Lake, as seen especially in No. 1, can be compared to that of Rankin artists such as Tiktak. According to Grenier, quoted in a biography of the artist in the files of the Department of Indian and Northern Affairs, Angaktaaryuaq made figurines, animals, and masks in clay. In a terracotta sculpture now in the collection of the Winnipeg Art Gallery (fig. 1), Angaktaaryuaq has concentrated on the subject of heads; here the fictile medium is fashioned into more rounded, modelled versions of his typical horizontal/vertical featured face.

Fig. 1.
Joseph Angaktaaryuaq (1935-1976) m.
Baker Lake (and Rankin Inlet)
Heads c. 1967
Terracotta
26.0 x 24.7 x 26.7 cm
The Winnipeg Art Gallery
Donated by the Women's Committee

2.
Joseph Angaktaaryuaq (1935-1976) m.
Mother and Child c. 1974
Black stone
10.5 x 10.0 x 5.5 cm
Unsigned
78/399

1.
Joseph Angaktaaryuaq (1935-1976) m.
Mother and Child c. 1973
Dark grey stone
13.0 x 6.3 x 7.4 cm
Signed with syllabics
78/642

1A

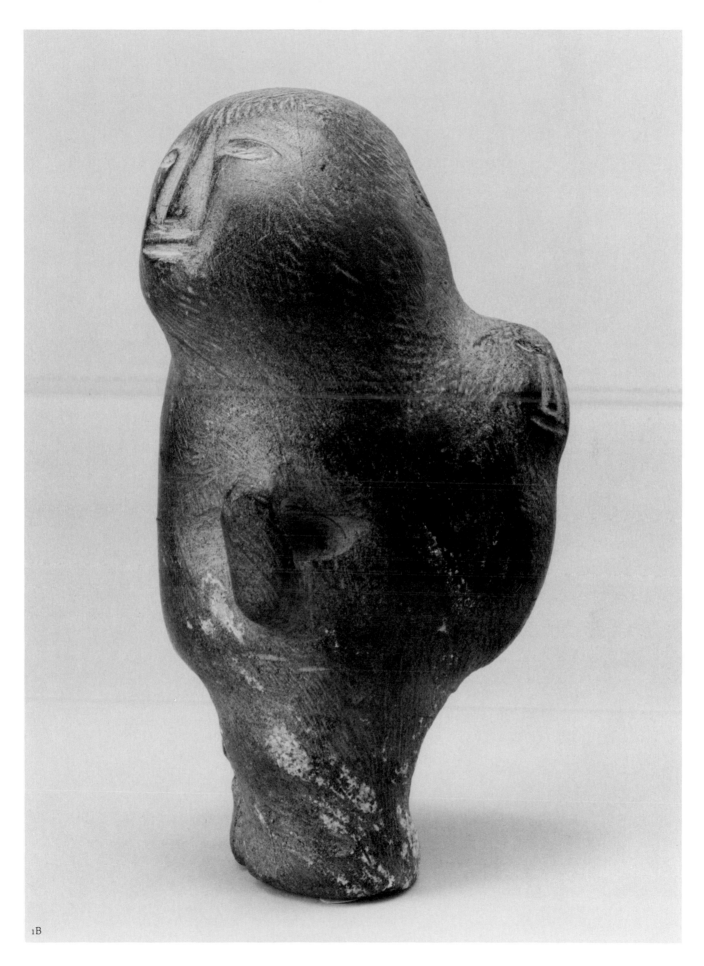

1B

LUKE ANGUHADLUQ

Anguhadluq began drawing in 1968 when he was in his early seventies. From then until his death in 1982 he continued to draw in his own distinctive style, recorded in some seventy prints published in Baker Lake print collections between 1970 and 1982.

From the beginning Anguhadluq seemed to have established his particular subject interests and his own way of conveying them from the three-dimensional world to two-dimensional paper. Economic of means, he suggested and abbreviated forms rather than extensively articulating them; he let the empty white areas of his paper work for him, never fearing to leave areas undisturbed (although conversely, he might completely fill the page with images or a background). He repeated forms or distorted them for realistic and visual effects, and he adjusted his perspective system to meet particular needs within his scene.

Made from a drawing from about 1968, the 1973 print *Fishing* (No. 7) is a good example of Anguhadluq's early work. Rudimentary fishermen figures with outstretched arms, but few other features, reach out to hold their fish spears, whose importance to the undertaking is signified by their size, which dwarfs the human beings. The perimeter of the fish lake is circumscribed with a single line; the mouth of the connecting stream is indicated with the opening to the right, but not, as in some drawings, continued into a thin straight line for the stream itself. Inside the lake the fish are oriented to their pursuers, making them seem upside down to us.

Anguhadluq was a respected hunter until unusually late in life and his graphic works reflect his life on the land where the important subjects are the hunt and the animals hunted. In hunting and fishing scenes, and in his depictions of geese, caribou, and other animals, we see his sensitive use of colour, his effective use of repetition, and his sense of humour. While the distribution of different coloured repetitive elements makes a balanced, pleasing composition in the page filled with a flock of geese flying overhead (No. 8), the single, upside-down kayaker in the group of kayaks (No. 3) provides an unexpected vision of a boating accident or, more likely, just humorous variation. Lifetime hunter that he was, he even distinguished between the winter and summer coats of the caribou, using a single line under the belly of the caribou (No. 6) to enclose its unprinted white underside.

Another popular subject in Anguhadluq's work is the single female figure. With her delicate face and braids, the inordinately broad shoulders of her child-carrying *amautiq*, and her attenuated arms, her feminine parka flap falling phallic-like between her sturdy columnar legs, Anguhadluq's *Woman* (No. 4) is an archetypal and primordial earth mother.

3.
Luke Anguhadluq (1895-1982) m.
Printed by Thomas Iksiraq (1941–) m.
Kayaks and Caribou 1971
Stonecut and stencil 38/46
62.7 x 100.3 cm
78/527

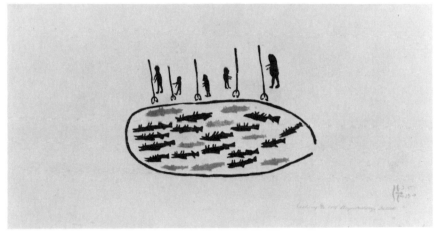

7.
Luke Anguhadluq (1895-1982) m.
Printed by Margaret Tullik (1942–) f.
Fishing 1973
Stonecut and stencil 6/50
26.1 x 48.8 cm

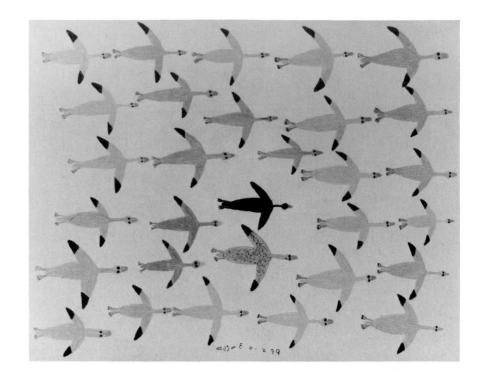

8.
Luke Anguhadluq (1895-1982) m.
Birds in Flight c. 1973
Coloured pencil and pencil
58.6 x 73.5 cm
Signed lower centre with syllabics and
    disc number
78/544

5.
Luke Anguhadluq (1895-1982) m.
Printed by Margaret Tullik (1942–) f.
April Caribou 1973
Stonecut and stencil 26/50
30.5 x 49.0 cm
78/533

6.
Luke Anguhadluq (1895-1982) m.
Printed by Margaret Tullik (1942–) f.
September Caribou 1973
Stonecut and stencil 36/50
30.4 x 48.8 cm
78/654

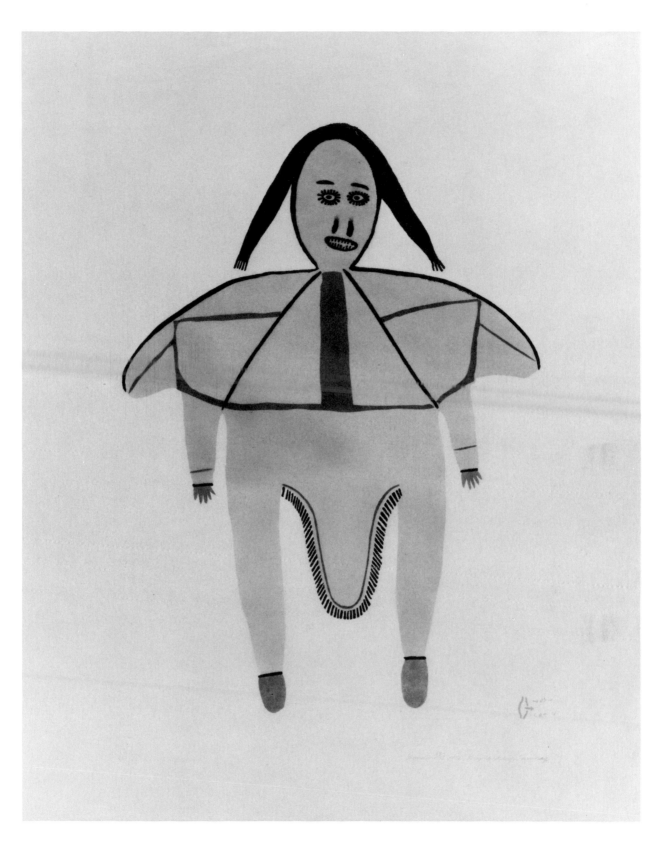

4.
Luke Anguhadluq (1895-1982) m.
Printed by Irene Taviniq (1934–) f.
Woman 1972
Stonecut and stencil 29/43
80.5 x 64.0 cm
78/529

The *Woman Holding Child* (No. 9), one of three carvings by Aqiggaaq included in the Masterworks exhibition (Canadian Eskimo Arts Council, *Sculpture/Inuit* No. 302), is a classic example of Baker Lake sculpture from the 1960s – the black stone, the subject matter, and its treatment are all typical.

Working with their stone, Baker Lake artists such as Aqiggaaq managed, even in small carvings, to convey a sense of monumentality. In this case the sculpture is not small, and the massiveness of the figure is achieved partly through actual size, but also through the tremendous width of the woman's shoulders, the breadth of her chest, the solidity of her stocky legs firmly planted on the ground, and the effortlessness with which she carries her child, his weight in no way throwing off her upright pose. All in all, it is an image to be compared with Anguhadluq's depiction of the female in his print *Woman* (No. 4).

Set into her parka hood, like a cameo, is the woman's dainty face, with its finely detailed features, hairline, and tattoo marks. Inclined and suppressed as it is, the face is a crowning, precious note complementing and rounding out the curves and flow of her handsome body.

9A

9.
Matthew Aqiggaaq (1940–) m.
Woman Holding Child 1967
Black stone
41.0 x 30.9 x 20.5 cm
Signed with syllabics
78/205

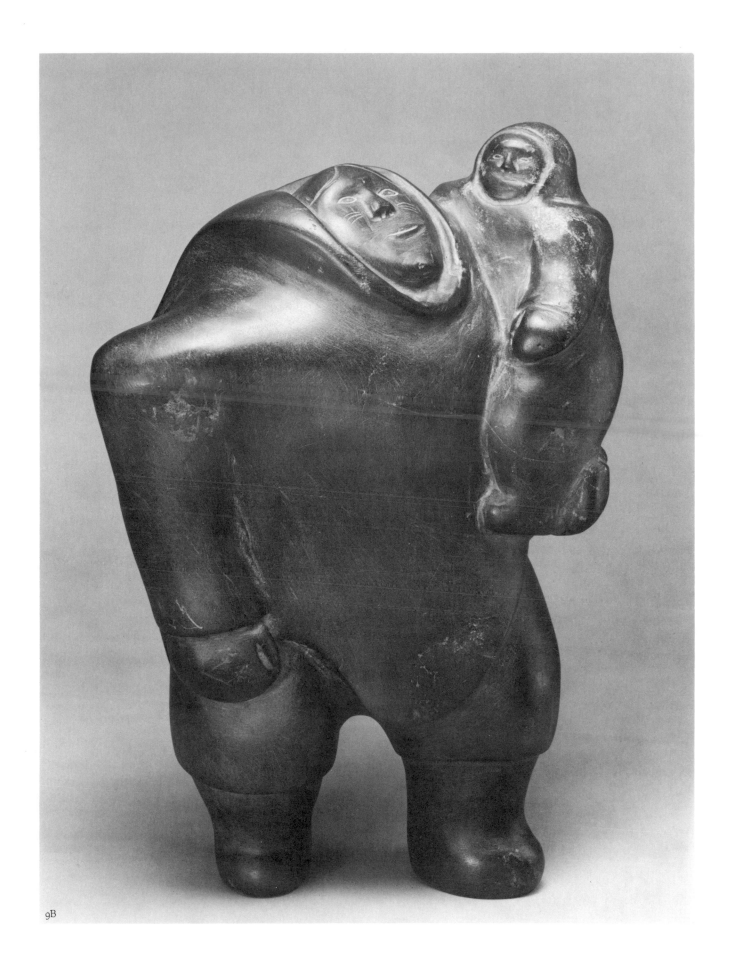

9B

IRENE AVAALAAQIAQ

The making of wall hangings is a fairly recent development, but one that utilizes the traditional sewing skills of Inuit women. Once responsible for making all the clothing and footwear for herself and her family, the seamstress now also turns her talents to the making of garments and sewings for sale. In addition to making standard articles of clothing, such as *kamiks,* mitts, and parkas for their southern customers, women in different settlements have made various types of sewn handicrafts such as stuffed dolls, handbags, and wall hangings.

Although work with hand-sewn pictures or scenes, made of wool, sealskin, or hide, has taken place sporadically over the years, in Baker Lake serious work in this medium began after the arrival of Jack and Sheila Butler in mid-1969 (see Introduction, p. 13). Since then the hangings from Baker Lake have been singled out, and justly so; the works, many impressive in size, are characterized by original images, sensitive compositions, bright colours, and, most important of all for the proud seamstresses, beautifully done stitchery.

To make their hangings the women either appliqué or inset designs into the background and then decorate them with embroidered motifs, the complexity and amount of embroidery depending on the inclination and talents of the originator. The hangings, generally made without preliminary drawing or plan, are in some cases too large to be viewed in full by the seamstress in her home where she works. As a result, the women may only see their sewing in its entirety when it is hung up for a showing in the school gymnasium, suspended from the roof of the cooperative building, or displayed on exhibition in the south.

Avaalaaqiaq's two wall hangings included here show her typical flowing forms and profile faces, characteristics that also appear in her drawings. In these colourful hybrid forms, legs, arms, and tails turn into creatures, bodies sprout heads, faces look out from the side of a figure, while fins, *kamiks,* parka trim, features, eyes and eyebrows are embroidered on. Of particular interest in *Transformations* (No. 11) is the insetting of the entire green area into the tan background.

Although Avaalaaqiaq is well known for her hangings, she also does the occasional carving, draws (there have been more than twenty of her prints published since 1975), and works as a printmaker in the Baker Lake printshop.

10.
Irene Avaalaaqiaq (1941–) f.
Transformations c. 1973
Wool, felt and embroidery floss
100.5 x 145.5 cm
Unsigned
78/568

11.
Irene Avaalaaqiaq (1941–) f.
Transformations c. 1973
Wool, felt, embroidery floss and thread
82.0 x 128.5 cm
Unsigned
78/569

10

11

LUKE IKSIKTAARYUK

Not many Inuit sculptors choose to work in caribou antler, and fewer still have specialized in this medium. Antler is used by artists for special effects, for realistic details such as the horns on a sculptural caribou (No. 72), for bases or other complementary functions, or simply for a change in pace, but it has never been used extensively as a sculptural medium on its own. Although there are many places with plentiful supplies of caribou antler, it would seem that in a lot of cases antler is used for the main body of the sculpture only if the preferred materials of stone, ivory, or whalebone are not readily available.

Antler as an artistic medium does have its drawbacks. The horns are a dull bone colour while the flat, thin curving shapes with multiple protusions leave little volume or leeway for the carver. Antler lacks the size and interesting colour and shape of whalebone, the "carveability" and richness of ivory, and the versatility of stone.

Some artists, however, have been able to work within the confines of this medium and even take advantage of the particular properties and characteristics of antler. Such is the case with Iksiktaaryuk, who has specialized in making carvings in caribou antler. Under his hand the antler becomes people, spirits, fishmen, mermaids, shamans, a dance scene, or even the elements of a necklace (Art Gallery of Ontario, *The People Within*, Nos. 77-89). Often the antler alone is sufficient for making the scene. Iksiktaaryuk ingeniously used the natural configuration of the antler to represent or suggest various shapes and forms: the spreading base area where the tip extends from the main trunk of the antler becomes the bulging back of a woman's parka; the different protrusions on the antler become the legs and tail of a spirit; the multi-tipped area of the antler becomes an elevated, open base; the knob at the root of the antler becomes the head of a figure; and the curving antler trunk becomes the body of a shaman in its dynamic, powerful thrust forward.

Some sculptures are made entirely out of a single piece of antler, perhaps with an added base; other times the subject may have attached arms, tail fins, or wings, all done in antler, of course. Sometimes other caribou products are added: caribou hair for the chest ornament of the shaman figure, caribou hide and little antler attachments for the shaman's belt, and caribou heart tissue for the head of the drum. More rarely, additional parts are made of other materials, but these tend to be used in less obvious places, such as the wooden rim for the drum and the inset nails used to peg the figures to their base.

Iksiktaaryuk's use of antler demonstrates not only his sensitivity to and ability to work with this difficult medium, but also his economy of means in doing so; for example, in the *Drum Dance* (No. 12) scene, the drummer's arm and the drum beater he holds are one piece of antler, the beater at the end of the piece separated from the arm with an incised dividing line. The same economic, almost austere, style is characteristic of Iksiktaaryuk's graphics, where lines are used to maximum effect. Sometimes the graphic will show a scene of drum dancing or a group of animals, but more often the subject is a sole bird or animal drawn with minimal line and colour, with perhaps some cross hatching or grouping of parallel lines for different textures. *The Great Owl* (No. 13), typical of his style, is one of fourteen Iksiktaaryuk graphics printed between 1970 and 1977.

12.
Luke Iksiktaaryuk (1909-1977) m.
Drum Dance c. 1974
Antler, wood, sinew, metal, and gut
16.4 x 32.6 x 40.7 cm
Unsigned
78/386

13.
Luke Iksiktaaryuk (1909-1977) m.
Printed by William Kanak (1937–) m.
The Great Owl 1973
Stonecut 37/50
53.0 x 65.8 cm
78/537

JANET KIGUSIUQ

With cut-away views of the igloo interiors and accompanying Inuktitut text, Kigusiuq shows us what she described in a recent interview as daily activities in a winter camp.

The syllabics in the upper right read: "Just came into camp," and the three upper igloos show domestic scenes; at the upper left two women prepare lengths of hide or sinew, the central woman seems to be scraping a skin as her husband offers a needle, while outside their igloo two figures prepare to crawl through the opening passage. At the upper right a mother with a child in her *amautiq* hands a water pail to the man. Below this igloo is an aerial view into another – here the text says: "Woman about to give birth to a child," and the scene shows a young woman crouched in childbirth attended by an older woman and, possibly, her husband (traditionally the attendants at birth were usually other women). To the left in another igloo a drum dance takes place – as the text states: "Drum dance in an igloo."

Below this dance scene in another igloo are a male and female figure with a lamp. As the text explains: "Brother and sister having hard time trying to keep the *kudlik* going, and when the light went out the boy kissed his sister." The result of which is described in the Inuktitut over the igloo entrance way: "Sister of the boy went out when she found out what her brother did to her."

Many of Kigusiuq's drawings are concerned with camp life, as well as spirits, legends, and transformation – subjects derived from her own experiences living on the land and from the stories and songs she has heard. Often included in these depictions are the realistic details and small incidents characteristic of events remembered from one's past. The hunting and camp scenes in particular are full of activities, sometimes occurring simultaneously, sometimes as a sequence of events showing a passage of time. The artist's use of several viewpoints, such as the aerial and side views into the different igloos in this drawing, is not at all unusual in her work or, for that matter, in Inuit graphic art in general.

Over twenty-five prints have been made from Kigusiuq's drawings since 1971. Kigusiuq, a daughter of Jessie Oonark, also makes wall hangings.

14.
Janet Kigusiuq (1926–) f.
Winter Camp Scene c. 1974
Pencil and coloured pencil
50.8 x 66.2 cm
Signed upper left with syllabics and disc
    number
78/560

MYRA KUKIIYAUT

Looking at Kukiiyaut's graphics is like looking into another world where colourful, undulating forms seem to float and flow over the surface of the paper in timeless space. This unstructured, dreamlike, often non-narrative style, with its emphasis on colour and shape, can be related to Kukiiyaut's subliminal drawing style: "I just start drawing and then it becomes different from what I thought I was going to draw. And one drawing leads to another" (1977 Baker Lake print catalogue, unpaged).

Kukiiyaut uses flat, broad areas of colour to define her forms – the figure may be outlined, but colour instead of line is used to articulate and distinguish different surface patterns and the shape of the subjects. The outline of the figures, often a curving continuous line, creates a sense of rhythmic flow across the surface while the broad areas of colour keep the figures flat.

The lack of depth or perspective is reinforced rather than alleviated by the placement of the figures on the page. Stacking images one above the other or overlapping them can be used to give some suggestion of three-dimensional space, but here the images remain close to the picture plane. The bird, animal, human, and transformed subjects in a Kukiiyaut drawing tend not to be oriented to a ground line either suggested or actually articulated. Not stabilized by a fixed point of reference on the white piece of paper the figures appear to be floating in space. This effect is heightened by the timelessness of many of the scenes where no locale or event is particularized.

As their titles indicate, some of Kukiiyaut's prints are concerned with narrative events such as *Drum Dance* (1974/28) or *Returning Hunters* (1981/23), but the dance is attended by floating heads and the returning hunters are legless, immobile forms with no sign of captured prey. Even in the more representational and specific event shown in *The Dying Man Becomes a Wolf* (1972/37), there is not just one point of orientation, but several, while the temporal sequence conveyed by the depiction of both the dying man and the wolf he will (has) become is rare in Kukiiyaut's work.

In discussing her drawings for the exhibition *Inuit Myths, Legends and Songs*, Kukiiyaut identified subjects derived from her own experiences and from her memory of traditional songs, legends, and beliefs. The titles of some of her prints such as *Dream, Dreaming,* and *Cloud Shapes,* however, suggest other sources and orientations. In an interview with the author in August 1972, Kukiiyaut explained that she looked for ideas for her drawings in floor dirt or stains, and in the sky.

Having quit drawing for a time in the late sixties. "because I drew the way everyone else did" (Driscoll, *Inuit Myths, Legends and Songs,* p. 43), Kukiiyaut since 1970 has worked in her own distinctive style. She has also made wall hangings, and between 1978 and 1981 she printed a number of her own graphics.

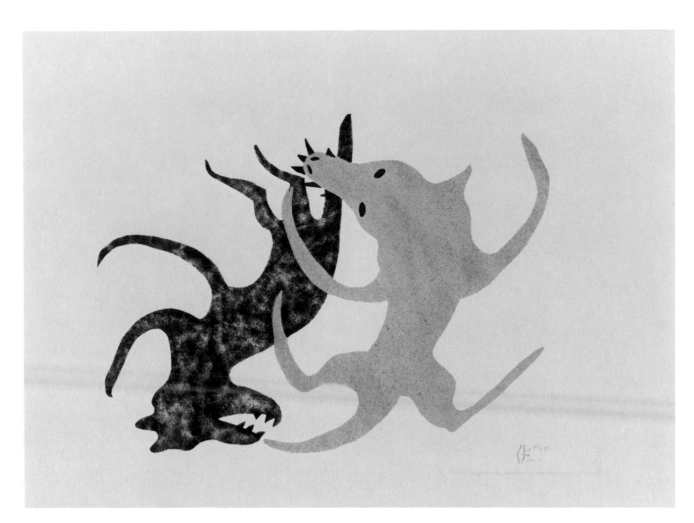

15.
Myra Kukiiyaut (1929–) f.
Printed by Phillipa Aningrniq (1944–) f.
The Dancing Wolf and His Shadow 1973
Stencil 6/50
56.0 x 76.4 cm
78/535

WILLIAM NOAH

In hunting cultures such as that of the traditional Inuit, bones seem to have held a special place of interest and importance. Hidden beneath the flesh during life, they remained intact far longer than flesh and blood after death. On a more practical level, the skeletal structure of the animals they hunted and butchered was an integral part of the hunting family's knowledge. In the art works of these people, the depiction of skeletal patterns, joint marks, or x-ray views of the bones within the human or animal body often had a magico-religious significance.

Vestiges of these skeletal markings, common in prehistoric Eskimo art, appear from time to time in contemporary sculpture and graphics (figs. 22-23, p. 191). Often, as in another work by William Noah of a skeletoned *Shaman* (1972/24), the markings appear in the context of shamanism, reflecting the shaman's ability to see himself as a skeleton during the initiation process and, as the all-seeing healer and guardian, to see into the body of his charges.

While William's skeletal representation in the *Shaman* and in another print *Spirit* (1971/33) certainly relates to shamanic belief, his *Skeletoned Caribou* (No. 17) and other representations of caribou such as *The Great Male Caribou* (fig. 2) and *Caribou Swimming in Sunset* (1975/4) concentrate on visual rather than religious concerns. The latter two works show William's great interest in landscape in a style influenced by comic books and westerns. Unlike the intensely coloured caribou shown against a plain white background in the print *Skeletoned Caribou*, the other two caribou move through a colourful landscape highlighted by the slanting rays of the setting sun.

Similarly in *Qiviuq's Journey* (No. 16), a complex printing job results in a colourful, albeit more subdued in tone, representation of an episode from the legend of Qiviuq, a Ulysses-like traveller whose many adventures included a journey over the water on the back of a fish. In this work and a number of others in the yearly Baker Lake collections, William and his wife Martha collaborated in the actual printing of his drawing. In other cases, such as *Skeletoned Caribou* (No. 17), William does his own printing; he also prints drawings done by other Baker Lake artists.

William is the son of Jessie Oonark. He, his sisters, and his mother suffered greatly after William's father died when William was still a youth – too young to provide for the others. After moving to Baker Lake, William attended school and then went to Winnipeg for a carpentry course. Returning to Baker Lake, he and Martha were married and he worked as a carpenter, a line man, and tried some carving. He first tried drawing in 1963, and then again in 1970. "In 1971," he recalls, "I walked down to the craft shop like a man and got myself a job as a printmaker" (1972 Baker Lake print catalogue, unpaged). Since then, in addition to drawing and printmaking, he has been active in community and Inuit affairs. He was President of the Sanavik Cooperative in Baker Lake from 1976 to 1980; a member and then Chairman of the Board of Directors of Canadian Arctic Producers, Ltd. in Ottawa; Chairman of the Baker Lake Hamlet Council; and Keewatin North member of the Territorial Council of the Northwest Territories. In 1978 he travelled to Houston, Texas to give a presentation on Inuit printmaking at the Institute of International Education's salute to Canada.

Fig. 2.
William Noah (1943–) m.
Baker Lake
The Great Male Caribou c. 1971
Coloured pencil
52.3 x 75.2 cm
The Winnipeg Art Gallery
Donated by Dr. and Mrs. E. G. Berry

16.
William Noah (1943–) m.
and Martha Noah (1943–) f.
Qiviuq's Journey 1973
Stonecut and stencil 6/50
64.0 x 94.0 cm
78/531
See colour plate on page 17.

17.
William Noah (1943–) m.
The Skeletoned Caribou 1974
Stonecut and stencil 22/35
63.5 x 94.4 cm
78/536

The first of the annual Baker Lake print collections was released in 1970, but the first Oonark prints were released ten years before this in the 1960 Cape Dorset print collection. Not only did Oonark begin drawing long before the arts and crafts program made this a popular art form in Baker Lake, but the quality of her work quickly provoked attention and encouragement. Through special arrangements with the Cape Dorset printshop, three prints were made from her drawings and released along with the annual Cape Dorset collections – two appeared in 1960, one in 1961. Oonark, whose name on these Dorset prints is spelled Una, has continued to be singled out for her artistic abilities, so evident in both her drawings and wall hangings.

Oonark – the mother of eight children including artists Janet Kigusiuq, William Noah, and Nancy Pukingrnak – is probably the best known of the Baker Lake artists. In addition to her participation in a number of exhibitions, group and solo, she has done illustrations for several books and received awards and commissions, including the commission for her very large wall hanging (c. 4 x 6 metres) that now hangs in the National Arts Centre in Ottawa. One of her hangings was presented to the Queen in 1973. In 1974 she was awarded best in the show for her hanging in the *Crafts from Arctic Canada* exhibition. In 1975 she was made a member of the Royal Canadian Academy, and in 1977 an honorary member of the Canadian Crafts Council.

The subjects – female figures and shamans with their helping spirits – in the four prints included here give little indication of the range of her subject matter which encompasses hunting, fishing, kayak and drum dance scenes, people, animals, various supernatural beings, even snow-mobiles and Christian subjects. Informative about specific traditional practices and beliefs, the prints included here are also good examples of her distinctive style – crisp, assured, balanced, and accomplished. Bold and direct, the images are often two-dimensional, emphasizing shapes and the overall compositional design. Many are colourful, but a limited palate can be used just as effectively.

In the print *Woman with Beautiful Hair* (No. 20), the woman's fancy hairdressing stands out in relief against the sensuous, bright red, hand-coloured background, while her posture suggests light-heartedness and gaiety. This print, its title in particular, and the print *Big Woman* (No. 21) convey to us a feminine concern for personal appearance among the Inuit women who traditionally did not use jewellery or make-up. Another form of adornment, in addition to elaborate hair-dos, was tattooing – faces, hands, even arms and thighs were decorated with black soot tattoo marks. The woman in *Big Woman* (No. 21), whose face is quite heavily tattooed, also has beautifully dressed hair. Two large stylized *ulus* (the woman's knife) to the sides of her head provide additional visual and compositional embellishments. Her body, quite small in comparison to her head and hair, maintains a supporting role compressed within the lower part of the image. The little figure on her head may represent her thoughts of a child or a child in the *amautiq* behind, although a spiritual inter-pretation might also be possible.

Certainly the little figure on top of the head of the shaman in *A Shaman's Helping Spirits* (No. 19) represents a spirit or the shaman's other persona. In this print and in the *Flight of the Shaman* (No. 18), the shaman's helping spirits appear both on and inside his body. Such was the close relationship between the shaman and his spirits; the spirits, often remaining close at hand to help their shaman as soon as the thought of them was formed, might perch on his head or shoulders or live in his mouth. In the print *Flight of the Shaman* one of the shaman's important abilities, flying, is graphically portrayed.

21.
Jessie Oonark (1906–) f.
Printed by Simon Tookoome (1934–) m.
Big Woman 1974
Stonecut and stencil 27/50
62.8 x 94.4 cm
78/167
See colour plate on page 18.

20.
Jessie Oonark (1906–) f.
Printed by Francis Kaluraq (1931–) m.
Woman with Beautiful Hair 1971
Stonecut and hand-coloured paper 37/37
48.5 x 61.0 cm
78/528

18.
Jessie Oonark (1906–) f.
Printed by Michael Amarook (1941–) m.
   and Martha Noah (1943–) f.
Flight of the Shaman 1970
Stonecut and stencil 22/50
52.0 x 66.8 cm
78/649

19. Opposite
Jessie Oonark (1906–) f.
Printed by Thomas Sivuraq (1941–) m.
A Shaman's Helping Spirits 1971
Stonecut and stencil 24/40
94.2 x 63.8 cm
78/165

Multi-headed creatures similar to the one in No. 22 appear in a number of Pukingrnak's drawings (Driscoll, *Inuit Myths, Legends and Songs*, pp. 72-75) and one is partially visible in the Pukingrnak print *The Spirit and the Wolf* (1982/23). The creature, identified in some titles as Qavavaq, is characterized by a double head, an additional two faces on its back, clawed hands and feet, and a tail terminating in a clawed hand. These creatures — one drawing shows both male and female varieties — are violent and bloodthirsty, preying on human beings whom they dismember and devour.

The creature in the sculpture illustrated on pages 60 and 61 also has a double head and two extra faces on his back, but he seems much less aggressive than the creatures in the drawings. Since he also lacks the typical ears and claws, and no tail is visible, perhaps he is not one of these man-eating beasts. It may be that the visual format but not the horrific connotations have surfaced here — the heads acting more as a sculptural motif. Or the heads may echo back to an episode in the popular myth about the legendary hero Qiviuq, another favourite subject of Pukingrnak's, where the journeying Qiviuq meets the woman Igutsaq (Epooptakjuak) who eats human beings, except for their heads which she stores in rows in her dwelling.

The drawing illustrated here (No. 23) shows another side to Pukingrnak's art work, that is, the intimate, domestic scene, busy with everyday concerns; the terrorizing creatures and horror of the unknown for the moment forgotten, or at least pushed to one side. Even Pukingrnak's graphic style becomes more delicate and gentle in keeping with the more idyllic atmosphere of the drawing. Certainly there is some hunting and shooting going on in this drawing but the attack on the musk-ox in the upper left and the scene in the lower left where men with bows and arrows shoot at a wolf are part of the daily hunting lifestyle. More unusual is that the men also seem to be shooting at the man near the wolf. Why they are doing so is not entirely clear; perhaps he is someone whose behaviour has made him dangerous to the others, perhaps he is an intruder and these are warning shots before he identifies himself as a friendly visitor.

Oblivious to this exchange the participants in the rest of the scene peacefully go about their business – one man smokes his pipe, another, with a little ground squirrel nearby, watches caribou through his telescope, a girl has her hair dressed, an older woman with tattoo marks on her face sings the monotonous lullaby of ai-yai-yai to a child held by its mother, and another woman works at preparing a skin inside her tent. In this tent and the one in the lower left we see various implements and interior furnishings. The little circles around the outside are the rocks which hold down the lower edges of the tent; a side view of them can be seen in a third tent at the upper left. In the centre and upper right of the drawing we see a fish weir, the captured fish carried by the fishermen to the women who clean and string them up to dry.

The drawing is full of minute and informative details such as the syllabics of the old woman's chant, the eyelashes on the charming little caribou, the cups, tea kettle, and other utensils inside the tents, the smoke from the man's pipe, and the tattoo marks on the faces of several women. Busy with these aspects we barely stop to notice the pencilled over area in the lower left which presumably covers a slip of the pencil. Mistakes of this

sort are surprisingly rare in drawings like this that are done extemporane-
ously without preliminary sketches or, in most cases, erasures. Generally
errors are covered over and/or converted into something else.

In addition to being a consummate draughtsman and carver (see also
Blodgett, *The Coming and Going of the Shaman*, No. 2 and The Winnipeg
Art Gallery, *The Zazelenchuk Collection of Eskimo Art*, No. 31), Pukingrnak,
the daughter of Jessie Oonark, also makes wall hangings. Although
Pukingrnak has been drawing for some years, prints made from her
drawings were not published until 1982.

23.
Nancy Pukingrnak (1940–) f.
Camp Scene c. 1974
Pencil and coloured pencil
50.5 x 66.0 cm
Signed lower centre right with syllabics
78/559

22A

22.
Nancy Pukingrnak (1940–) f.
Figure with Faces 1974
Black stone
14.0 x 7.8 x 13.3 cm
Signed with syllabics and dated
78/626

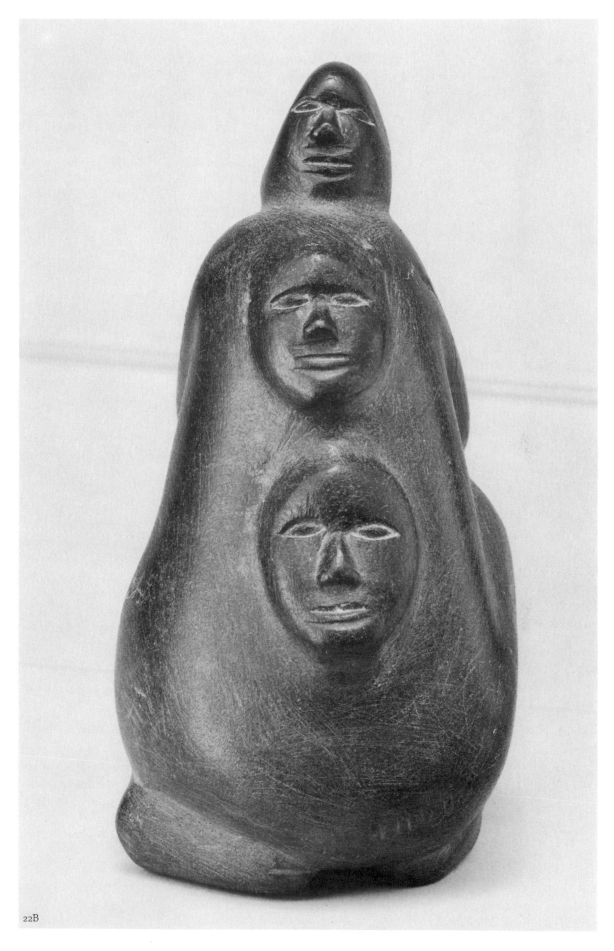

22B

Were it not for the tusks protruding from the mouth of one of the figures in *Shaman Transformation* (No. 24), this sculpture might be mistaken for a mother and her child. The nestling of the two figures together within a protective, sheltering form gives an air of intimacy and security to the work. Yet, this subtle, unassuming air belies a multiplicity of shamanistic undertones.

Although the shaman or *angakoq* of traditional Eskimo belief had special innate powers which set him apart from his fellow human beings and enabled him to act as an intermediary between this world and the supernatural, he also underwent a period of training with an established shaman. His novitiate often occurred when he himself was just becoming an adult, and his relationship to the master was in many ways like that of a child to a parent. The older shaman instructed, showed by example, nurtured and spiritually raised the shaman-to-be, and the closeness of their relationship, their mutual trust, and the dependence of the younger person on the elder is visually signified by their presentation both literally and symbolically as mother and child. Additionally, although the office of shaman was not hereditary, shamanic qualities tended to run in families, and the elder would often instruct his own offspring.

This shamanic relationship is the subject of several similar sculptures: Davidialuk's *Woman Shaman and Apprentice in Tent* (fig. 3) and Karoo Ashevak's *Coming and Going of the Shaman* (fig. 4). In the Ashevak, sculptural indications, such as the two different sizes of hands, distinguish this from a straightforward representation of a mother and child. This interpretation is substantiated by Karoo's explanation that the sculpture is a representation of the transference of shamanic power from the older shaman (whose larger head and hand are made of darker, more porous whalebone) to the younger (whose smaller head and hand are made of a lighter coloured, denser whalebone). In the Davidialuk sculpture, as in the Sivuraq, the tusks signify the shaman, since during séances his transformation might involve the growth of large teeth from his mouth (ivory false teeth for shamanic performances date from as early as prehistoric cultures). Similar shamanic teeth appear in another Sivuraq sculpture *Shamans and Animals* (Blodgett, *The Coming and Going of the Shaman*, No. 166), dated a year earlier than this one.

As the title of the Davidialuk sculpture indicates, women as well as men could become shamans. The image of woman shaman and neophyte as mother and child, then, seems doubly appropriate, yet neither the Ashevak nor the Sivuraq clearly indicates the sex of the shaman or the child. If the Ashevak format is obviously that of a woman with a child in her *amautiq*, the facial features tell us nothing of their sex; in the Sivuraq the two figures are simply nestled together as we often see them in mother and child sculptures, but again their sex is not clearly indicated. Such a distinction may seem unnecessary within the broader impact of the general subject, but it may also be related to other shamanic characteristics.

Duality was an important aspect of the shaman's existence. In his roles as intermediary between mankind and the supernatural, as protector and healer, and as the all-seeing, all-knowing guide for his charges, he could not only transform himself, but he was also shaman and human, human and animal, human and spirit, even male and female. The duality of the shaman is sometimes represented in works by a figure and a second face, or a double figure. Certainly the figure with the tusks in the Sivuraq sculpture looks the younger of the two and is slightly lower and

Fig. 3.
Davidialuk Alasua Amituk (1910-1976) m.
Povungnituk
Woman Shaman and Apprentice in Tent c. 1962
Dark grey stone
23.3 x 34.7 x 12.3 cm
Eskimo Museum, Churchill

Fig. 4.
Karoo Ashevak (1940-1974) m.
Spence Bay
Coming and Going of the Shaman c. 1973
Whalebone, antler, and stone
38.5 x 26.6 x 29.1 cm
George Sutherland, Spence Bay

24.
Thomas Sivuraq (1941–) m.
Shaman Transformation 1975
Dark grey stone and bone
26.0 x 24.6 x 14.0 cm
Signed with syllabics and dated
78/736

subordinate to the other figure, but it is almost the same size, and neither figure is identified as male or female. Perhaps then, the two figures symbolize all these things: the mother and child, the elder and neophyte shaman, the male and female, the human and spiritual. Such multi-levels of interpretation and subtle, even ambiguous symbolism are not unusual in art works related to shamanism.

In the 1977 Baker Lake print catalogue Tookoome is quoted as saying: "I am having a hard time printing my own drawings because they are so complicated" (1977 Baker Lake print catalogue, unpaged). Acting as printmaker as well as draughtsman, Tookoome usually prints his own drawings, unlike most artists whose drawings are transferred into prints by the printshop staff. That Tookoome should undertake to print his own complicated drawings, difficult for a printer to render on the printing stone, is fortunate since his printing abilities are so obviously equal to his drawing style. His prints, drawn and printed as they are by one person, are distinctly his – bold, colourful, strong, and expressive.

Moving into the settlement of Baker Lake in 1965 Tookoome, after working with the Department of Transport and a summer construction crew, approached the Craft Shop "to see if I could do something" (1973 Baker Lake print catalogue, unpaged). He did some drawing first and then began work at the printshop. Since 1970 when *The Pleasures of Eating Fish* (No. 25) was printed (it was released in 1971), he has continued to produce his own prints for the yearly Baker Lake collections.

Working at the Craft Shop offered Tookoome, an ardent hunter renowned for his handling of the twenty-foot-long dog whip, the advantages of a steady job while still allowing him a great degree of freedom, both in the flexible working hours that permitted hunting trips, but also through participation in group decision-making. Even before it was incorporated as the Sanavik Cooperative, the Baker Lake Craft Shop in the early 1970s was a cooperative venture; prints being made by one person, for example, were discussed by all the staff in a weekly meeting. Describing the cooperative in a 1976 interview with Kay Kritzwiser while in Toronto for the exhibition *The People Within* (at the Art Gallery of Ontario) in which he participated, Tookoome said: "Where Eskimo expression in the arts is concerned, no one else interferes."

While the Inuit may make their own decisions and even influence local and national native affairs through the cooperative, their art making itself remains a viable means of personal expression. In some areas of the Arctic the missionaries' discouragement of traditional religious beliefs – including their ban on séances, other practices, and even talk about shamanism – somehow did not encompass the making of art works. The Inuit, loathe to discuss or acknowledge shamanism, will nevertheless draw or carve explicit, revealing representations of shamanic practices. Such is certainly the case in Baker Lake, from whence come some of the most informative and successful shamanic works.

A number of Tookoome's graphics directly illustrate religious beliefs or indirectly reflect them. All three prints illustrated here include such shamanistic elements as transformation, spirits, and duality or multiplicity. The man jigging for fish has a mask-like face and animal feet, while human and animal heads appear along the length of his arm; perhaps these elements signify a shaman or, simply, his aid to the fishermen and hunters. In *I Am Always Thinking About the Animals* (No. 26) it may be a hunter, like Tookoome himself, whose thoughts of animals sprout from his head while his three-part face looks in all directions, as though continually searching for game. The animals and humans around him could also represent the shaman's central role in helping the hunters in their pursuit of game through his intermediary role between the world of humans and that of the animals.

For as the title of the print *The World of Man and the World of Animals Come Together in the Shaman* (No. 27) states, the shaman is an interconnecting force between the two worlds. Tookoome illustrates the shaman's intermediary role and his ability to be both human and animal by giving him one human foot and one animal one. His bird-like wings enclose animal and human heads that are earthly, spiritual, or both. The dual, even multiple, nature of the shaman is also shown in his face, primarily two facing profiles, but also a third frontal face created by the profiles of the other two.

The visual play on the shaman's face is characteristic of Tookoome's penchant for the visual double entendre. Individual features are combined to create yet another effect, while background areas which would normally be negative spaces are filled in and pulled forward to act as positive ones. Tookoome has a strong sense of composition, and the images, many with central focus, are balanced or symmetrical. Although he can very effectively utilize bold, bright colours in his prints, he may also just as successfully do a monochrome linear depiction such as *Wave* (1971/5).

25.
Simon Tookoome (1934–) m.
The Pleasures of Eating Fish 1970
Stonecut and stencil 25/50
64.3 x 94.5 cm
78/650
See colour plate on page 21.

26.
Simon Tookoome (1934–) m.
I Am Always Thinking About the Animals
    1973
Stonecut and stencil 39/50
54.5 x 78.6 cm
78/538

27.
Simon Tookoome (1934–) m.
The World of Man and the World of
  Animals Come Together in the Shaman 1973
Stonecut and stencil 41/50
64.0 x 85.0 cm
78/170

With colourful embroidered rays extending out from her face, an *ulu* above and below her, the *Sun Woman* (No. 28) is surrounded by a plentiful world of animals, birds, and transformed creatures. While birds fly out to the corners of the scene, and intervening animals move this way and that in the open space, the creatures on the circle around her face proceed in an orderly fashion, oriented to their circular ground line. This circle, which circumscribes the area of the rays, provides a stabilizing line of attraction for the subjects and focusses attention on the central motif.

The woman's face is surrounded by different brightly coloured wedges that are in turn decorated with embroidery. While the animals have some surface detailing done with embroidery – scales on the fish, feathers on the bird – the area around the face is heavily worked in repetitive tear-drop shapes. This format of female face with coloured surrounding rays can be seen in the drawing *Woman's Face* by Tuu'luq (Blodgett, *Tuu'luq/Anguhadluq*, No. 13), while the treatment in this hanging is very similar to her beadwork, especially as seen in the decoration on a beaded *atteegee* made in 1971 (fig. 5). Although this particular garment was made recently, beadwork had been used for years by Inuit women to decorate their parkas.

The Butlers (see Introduction, p. 13), not long after their arrival in Baker Lake in 1969, instigated several beading projects to encourage the women's traditional skills, and to make use of supplies left over from an earlier beadwork program. (Arts and crafts officers in the north have to be inventive and make use of everything since getting supplies is still a problem, involving the wait for the yearly ship or the expense of paying air freight. In the early days in Cape Dorset, the Houstons gave their government office typing paper to draughtsmen, while in recent years when essential vinyl lacquer was missing from their order from the south, the lithographers bought out the Hudson's Bay Company store's supply of nail polish so they could keep printing.) Tuu'luq's beadwork was singled out by the Butlers, and when she began making wall hangings, her beading expertise found a new form of expression. The sewings of duffle and felt were enriched with bead-like embroidery decoration, and in some cases her sewn motifs became as abstract as beadwork often is.

In this wall hanging (No. 28) several of the fish-like creatures have human faces. Beings of this kind and even more unusual combinations of forms are common in Tuu'luq's hangings, as well as in her drawings. They reflect a traditional belief in transformation and the world of spirits; not only could humans and animals change form, but the variety of spirit creatures in the north is endless.

Tuu'luq and her husband Anguhadluq were featured in a two-man exhibition at the Winnipeg Art Gallery in 1976.

Fig. 5.
Beaded *atteegee* made by Marion Tuu'luq in 1971.
Collection of Mr. and Mrs. K. J. Butler, on loan to the Winnipeg Art Gallery.

28.
Marion Tuu'luq (1910–) f.
Sun Woman 1975
Wool, felt, embroidery floss and thread
127.0 X 183.0 cm
Signed lower centre with syllabics
78/670
See colour plate on page 29.

ANIRNIK OSHUITOQ

Strange scenes are not uncommon in Anirnik's work. To date nine prints have been published from Anirnik drawings. The subject matter in her works ranges from birds, animals, and quasi-representational compositions, to traditional scenes of creatures, spirits, and shamans to inexplicable scenes of strange humans and animals. Just what *is* represented in Anirnik's print *The Oracle* (fig. 6) or in her drawing *Figure and Animals* (No. 29)?

An examination of Anirnik drawings at the Cooperative in Cape Dorset suggests that her images are the result of an inquisitive, active mind that not only stores up actual visual images she has seen but that also creates new images from a mere suggestion of a subject or shape. Her drawing style is organic and intuitive, and one can see how the forms grow and change to fill in the page – bumps become faces, extremities grow into creatures. There are many strange beings in her drawings, some not unlike the one in *Figure and Animals* (No. 29). There are also many different kinds of hats or head decorations, including live ones such as fish and birds; sometimes the decoration seems to be long, flowing hair.

The curious effects created by fish on heads or animal extremities in Anirnik's drawings are accentuated by the appearance of images which are not only not traditionally Inuit, but which are totally unexpected in the north, such as a figure on a camel, another with flowing hair or hat carrying a staff-like object in his hand, a figure seated at a piano, and people on skis. As unlikely as it may seem at first, all of these images could have been seen by Anirnik in illustrations or in real life. Born aboard the *Active* and living near Lake Harbour, Anirnik, like most Inuit in this area, had contact with white people, their books and religion, as well as with the Lapland reindeer herders who worked (often on skis) at Amadjuak (between Cape Dorset and Lake Harbour on south Baffin Island) in the early 1920s.

Such exposure to the outside world was not unusual; what is more unusual is Anirnik's retention of these images and their reappearance on paper years later. It would appear that these many different visual images were stored in Anirnik's mind to resurface later, probably without conscious thought, so that disparate images are joined together without concern for their association, thus resulting in such strange combinations of images as in the two works illustrated here.

Fig. 6.
Anirnik (1902–) f.
Printed by Eegyvudluk (1931–) m.
The Oracle 1966
Stonecut and stencil
37.0 x 52.8 cm

29.
Anirnik (1902–) f.
Figure and Animals 1968
Coloured pencil
50.8 x 65.7 cm
Signed lower left with syllabics; dated on
  verso by Cooperative
78/546

Aside from a certain amount of wing flapping, the birds in this print (No. 30) do not seem too frightened by the bears behind them. And probably rightly so, since the indicators in the image counteract any sense of fear or impending attack. Even though the birds' wings are upraised, suggesting flight, their feet remain down and oriented to a ground area. The symmetry and ordered arrangement of objects in the image also creates a stable and static composition – the bears seem permanently fixed in place, never able to get one step closer to the birds. Perhaps the two large birds are bigger because they are closer to us, but within the context of the print their size also helps to keep the bears, all of which are smaller, at bay. Finally the bright, happy colours assure us that the birds are not in any great danger.

This colourful, cheerful style is characteristic of Anna's work, even though she experienced considerable personal loss and illness during her own lifetime. Tuberculosis and surgery necessitated several trips to hospital in the south. In the early 1960s, after the death of her husband in the south where they had both been in hospital, Anna, without close relatives in Lake Harbour where she had lived, joined her sisters in Cape Dorset where she lived until her death in 1971.

This print was originally attributed to Jamasie by mistake and his name appears in the chop and in the inscription on the print and as the credit in the print catalogue. Counting this print, now known to be hers, there have been eight Anna prints produced between 1968 and 1973. The works depict family scenes, animals, and compositions of a static and pleasant nature. There is nothing abrupt or untoward in them. As in this print the mysteries of the spiritual world and the dangers of this world are kept at bay in her bright and colourful compositions.

30.
Anna (1911-1971) f.
Printed by Ottochie (1904-1982) m.
Birds Frightened by Bears 1973
Stonecut and stencil 41/50
62.1 x 86.0 cm
78/513

AQJANGAJUK SHAA

Fig. 7.
Aqjangajuk Shaa (1937–) m.
Cape Dorset
Kneeling Figure c. 1970
Green/black stone
41.3 X 35.9 X 27.0 cm
Art Gallery of Ontario
Gift of the Klamer Family, 1978

Fig. 8.
Aqjangajuk Shaa (1937–) m.
Cape Dorset
Woman Holding Ulu c. 1966
Green stone
32.0 X 23.0 X 15.0 cm
Macmillan-Bloedel Limited, Vancouver

Fig. 9.
Aqjangajuk Shaa (1937–) m.
Printed by Iyola (1933–) m.
Cape Dorset
Wounded Caribou 1961
Stonecut
32.3 X 38.0 cm

Stylistically quite different, these two sculptures (Nos. 31 and 32) are nevertheless comparable to other works by Aqjangajuk. While certain characteristics in the two, such as the type of hands and facial structure, indicate a common authorship, their sculptural differences indicate that the artist is versatile and innovative.

Although it dates to about three years later than the *Figure with Ulu* (No. 31), the *Kneeling Woman with Boot* (No. 32) is by far the more traditional of the two. The subject and pose of this sculpture are reminiscent of the classic carvings of the 1950s from Inukjuak (Nos. 116, 118) which show warm, motherly women working at domestic chores. Certainly there is a calm, secure, and gentle feel to this sculpture – the stability and restfulness of the pose resulting from the manner in which the substantial bulk of the figure firmly rests low to the ground on the woman's legs folded under her body, their spacing forming a broad base. The attractiveness of the whole is created and reinforced by the sensuous curves, the lustrous beautifully braided hair, the facial features, and the rich dark green colour of the stone with its high polish.

This sculptural solidity and compactness can also be seen in other Aqjangajuk works such as the *Kneeling Figure* (fig. 7), featured at the artist's solo exhibition at the Innuit Gallery in 1970, and to a lesser degree, in a piece comparable to the *Figure with Ulu*, the *Woman Holding Ulu* (fig. 8) which was included in the Masterworks exhibition. Dated about 1966 the *Woman Holding Ulu* shows a standing Inuit woman, dressed in a parka, holding a large *ulu* in one hand. The theme of a figure holding an *ulu* relates to No. 31, but the treatment of this subject differs considerably. In spite of the disproportionately large *ulu*, the Masterworks sculpture remains basically traditional and unremarkable in format, in contrast to the sculptural license evident in the Klamer piece. Yet the two sculptures date to within a year of one another.

That Aqjangajuk is interested in the potential of his subject and his media can be seen in other works dating any time from the early 1960s to the present. Several illustrations in George Swinton's book *Sculpture of the Eskimo* (p. 189) show unusual transformed spirit creatures in poses and sculptural configurations that are challenging to the stone medium and artist alike. Another illustration shows a section of ivory tusk incised with a scene of several fallen caribou and their four-legged predators (dog or wolf); the subject and its treatment is similar to that in his 1961 print *Wounded Caribou* (fig. 9), the only Aqjangajuk graphic published to date. By distorting and exaggerating the caribou form, Aqjangajuk goes beyond a simple representation of a hunted animal to a dramatic and expressive representation of a creature in the throes of death.

In the sculpture *Figure with Ulu* (No. 31) the expressive qualities are channeled into a vital, energetic image. The figure in this sculpture is quite flat and two-dimensional, focussing attention on the front and back, particularly the former, while the centre area of the figure remains flat and undistinguished, focussing attention on the more detailed extremities. This outward thrust is reinforced by the stance: the outstretched knees and upraised arms as well as the v-shape created by the positioning of the feet and the bending legs give an impression of coiled energy, of potential upward and outward movement. The neckless head, squashed down as it is, adds to the sense of dynamic energy. The base of the v is stabilized by the outwardly-turned feet while the outward movement is contained by the arresting details of fingernails, the unusually large hand with spread fingers, and the thinly curved wedge of the *ulu* blade.

The presence of an *ulu*, the woman's knife, would suggest that the figure is a female, yet the lack of bodily definition, heavy masculine features, and lack of hair on the head – so different from the *Kneeling Woman with Boot* (No. 32) – confuse the identification. Such fine distinctions are obviously secondary to that of the sculptural image as a whole; Aqjangajuk focusses our attention on the expressive qualities of movement and energy, on the outline silhouette of the image, and on the interaction of form with intersecting spaces.

31.
Aqjangajuk Shaa (1937–) m.
Figure with Ulu c. 1967
Green stone
38.5 x 47.0 x 6.0 cm
Signed with syllabics
78/199
See colour plate on back cover.

31B

32.
Aqjangajuk Shaa (1937–) m.
Kneeling Woman with Boot c. 1970
Dark green-black stone
24.5 x 24.7 x 26.8 cm
Signed with syllabics
78/705

ELEESHUSHE PARR

In this drawing (No. 33) Eleeshushe presents an aerial view of the return-ing hunters pulling their boat up on to shore with the assistance of those waiting to welcome them – and their catch – home. Eleeshushe's perspective here can be compared to that of Anguhadluq of Baker Lake; the side view of figures upside down and right side up as well as the top view of the boat are all consistently organized around a central focal point to give a coherent, in-depth view of a scene of action on the ground below. All the figures on both sides of the boat are oriented head first toward the centre of activity making some of them appear to be upside down.

Using a western style wooden boat and rifles, the hunters have caught a number of seals, all neatly stacked in the bottom of their boat, a tidy arrangement not likely in the excitement and work of the hunt, but perhaps more indicative of the artist's own sense of order. The bright colour and festive air are compatible with the anticipation of the culinary delights to be had from such a good catch.

Eleeshushe, the wife of Parr (Nos. 74-79), was recognized in Cape Dorset for her ability to design and sew the elaborate traditional skin garments with their contrasting inset patterns. She began drawing in the early days of printmaking at Cape Dorset and occasionally made carvings. Of the six prints made from her drawings, two, *End of the Hunt* (1968/23) and *Walrus Hunt* (1970/40), portray boat-hunting scenes, the former similar to the drawing illustrated here.

33.
Eleeshushe (c. 1896-1975) f.
Returning from the Seal Hunt c. 1968
Coloured pencil
50.8 x 64.6 cm
Signed lower right with syllabics
78/175

JAMASIE TEEVEE

The selection of prints included here (Nos. 34-40) gives a good indication of Jamasie's style and choice of subject matter. In his work Jamasie consciously avoids modern scenes or equipment; instead he says, he concentrates on subjects which show something about the traditional Inuit. Jamasie's two main subjects are people and animals. Some works show just animals grouped together, others show two or three standing figures, but the majority illustrate traditional, everyday scenes and activities such as camps, igloo interiors, games, and different hunting techniques. Jamasie prints are lessons in hunting skills – pursuing sea animals in kayaks and *umiaks*, fighting off attacking bears, trapping foxes in high stone traps, corralling and spearing fish in weirs, and driving geese, unable to fly while moulting, into stone pens. The particular hunting technique is clearly illustrated as are the implements and equipment needed for each. Taken together they form an illustrated guide to traditional hunting practices.

The same careful attention afforded to the hunting scenes is also given to domestic ones, particularly details of clothing and equipment. For example, the small but accurately portrayed set of hunting implements in the lower right of the *Camp Scene* (No. 34) and the utensils *Inside the Igloo* (No. 36). Shown in the latter print, on the right near a dead seal soon to be eaten, is a traditional stone lamp above which a pair of decorated *kamiks* dry on a rack. On the other side of the igloo is a knife and another lamp. Near this, or perhaps above it, is a fish in a pot.

Unique among Jamasie's prints is the engraving *Taleelayo and Friends* (No. 40); none of his other prints represents a spiritual or mythological subject. A powerful goddess who resided beneath the sea, Taleelayo controlled the animals that were so important to the Inuit people. In this print her relationship with the northern animals is graphically illustrated. Supported by two musk-oxen, she in turn provides support for a stack of arctic animals.

The structure in this print (No. 40) is characteristic of one compositional technique in Jamasie's work. Two basic trends are evident in Jamasie's graphics. On the one hand are the prints showing various activities with a lot of action – people chasing, running, and moving about. On the other hand are the prints which are static, highly structured, and carefully organized. In these prints the people and animal subjects are lined up, spaced out, and fitted together with no overlapping – sometimes like interlocking pieces in a puzzle, other times like building blocks as in *Animals of Novoojuak* (No. 39; Novoojuak is an Inuit camp north of Cape Dorset). This interconnecting style can also be seen in the work of other artists such as Kenojuak (Nos. 47-54) and may result in part from a common drawing procedure in which the artist, without doing preliminary drawings or even without thinking ahead, will just begin drawing; the images simply emerge, as though of their own volition. Also like Kenojuak, Jamasie draws the outline of his image first and then fills it in.

This static style and Jamasie's limited subject matter make his images somewhat repetitive; yet they are never exactly the same. He himself has explained that the different colours and details in a drawing were used to provide variety. Thus Jamasie uses colour, markings, and other techniques to give variety to his basic subjects both within and between individual works. Particularly noticeable in his engravings is his use of different incising patterns to distinguish textures and details. His technical expertise in this is evident in the print *Taleelayo and Friends* (No. 40) – in the fur of the animals, the fins, hair, and lovely braid of the sea goddess, and in the delicately jagged outline around her elegant, long, thin body.

Approximately 100 Jamasie prints have been included in Cape Dorset yearly collections since 1964/65. Of these about one half are engravings, a medium that Jamasie has clearly mastered. Jamasie also makes the occasional sculpture, having started carving in the late 1950s. He began drawing in the early 1960s, as he says, after Terry Ryan came to Dorset (see Introduction, p. 13).

34.
Jamasie (1910–) m.
Camp Scene 1964
Engraving 13/50
31.5 X 45.5 cm
78/313

36.
Jamasie (1910–) m.
Inside the Igloo 1966
Engraving 3/50
25.3 x 32.8 cm
78/324

35.
Jamasie (1910–) m.
Chasing Geese into Stone Pen 1965
Engraving 3/50
31.6 x 45.1 cm
78/327

37.
Jamasie (1910–) m.
The Fish Weir 1971
Engraving 41/50
38.5 x 32.4 cm
78/492

39.
Jamasie (1910–) m.
Printed by Ottochie (1904-1982) m.
Animals of Novoojuak 1973
Stonecut 27/50
61.9 x 86.3 cm
78/518

40.
Jamasie (1910–) m.
Taleelayo and Friends 1973
Engraving 22/50
31.9 x 44.9 cm
78/519

38.
Jamasie (1910–) m.
Printed by Lukta (1928–) m.
Summer Games 1973
Stonecut 26/50
61.1 x 85.8 cm
78/509

Captured as it turns and dives in flight, Joanassie's bird displays a full wing span of beautifully polished green stone (No. 41). The innovative pose of the bird in this work is unusual in contemporary Inuit sculpture and strikingly effective. With its flattened head, stretching down at an angle, and the smooth, slightly dished expanse of back and spread wings, the viewer forgets that the lower wing of this heavy stone bird rests on the ground. Instead we see a bird, as it would appear from the ground looking upward, wheeling and diving in the sky. The thrust of the sculpture is to the thin wedge of the upper wing that slices through the air and along to the head which dives down and forward. The effect of flight and thus lack of great weight is emphasized by the way the sculpture rests on the ground, supported by another thin wing edge, echoing the one in the air above, and by the thin tip of the feathery tail.

A *Winged Head* (fig. 10) by Joanassie in the Twomey Collection at the Winnipeg Art Gallery shows a similar sculptural approach in the way the eyes are detailed and in the angular, crisp edges of the wings, but it has none of the dynamic movement so successfully conveyed in this bird. The *Winged Head* and a sculpture of a *Woman and Children*, also in the Winnipeg Art Gallery (*Cape Dorset*, No. 20), illustrate Joanassie's earlier sculptural style and subject matter. In later years he concentrated on bird subjects, especially since the late 1970s when he and the artist Kenojuak were married. From then until his death in 1981 sculptures by the two showed considerable cross influence.

Fig. 10.
Joanassie Igiu (1923-1981) m.
Cape Dorset
Winged Head 1962
Green stone
18.8 x 26.6 x 13.3 cm
The Jerry Twomey Collection, The
    Winnipeg Art Gallery – with
    appreciation to the Province of
    Manitoba and the Government of
    Canada

41. Opposite
Joanassie Igiu (1923-1981) m.
Bird in Flight c. 1976
Green stone
27.5 X 41.1 X 15.0 cm
Signed with syllabics
78/627

KANANGINAK POOTOOGOOK As President of the West Baffin Eskimo Cooperative in Cape Dorset for a number of years, Kananginak has been called upon to make introductory comments for several annual print catalogues. These statements and other discussions of his work give us some valuable insights into Kananginak the man and the artist. A producing artist and printmaker, Kananginak is a firm supporter of the cooperative movement through which, as he says, people can help themselves. He also takes an active interest in local affairs.

Such a life was not what the young Kananginak expected as a boy:

> In those days the idea of having to work for our livings never occurred to us, all I thought about was growing up to be a man, having a team of fast dogs and being able to get all the game I needed. However, I did not in the end travel by dog team for all that many years, for despite what I would have liked to do, there were more and more Kadlunaks [white people] arriving.
>
> (1973 Cape Dorset print catalogue, unpaged)

Instead Kananginak settled in Cape Dorset with his aging father, the great camp leader Pootoogook, and went to work for James Houston in 1958, first at odd jobs, then doing printmaking. Since that time Kananginak has printed other artists' drawings as well as his own – something that is not common in Cape Dorset where the role of draughtsman and printer are usually separate and distinct.

Although Kananginak has not lived full-time on the land since the 1950s, he is still an Inuk hunter. As he says, "I don't really want to go back to the old days. But when you think of the old days, it makes you proud – just to think of them" (1978 Cape Dorset print catalogue, p. 46). And his graphics generally reflect the animals, birds, and camp life of earlier times. In his prints, he shows how things are done – making a kayak, building a snow house, skinning a caribou, stretching a hide. In some works such as *All That We Own* (1975/63) the implements and equipment are carefully laid out and illustrated as though recording for posterity the belongings of traditional Inuit. This is certainly the case in Kananginak's illustrations of traditional activities:

> We like to keep our culture through carvings and prints. Those art pieces are very valuable; they tell of the past. . . . The artists and the hunters work very hard to keep this tradition going even though we have been introduced to new writing systems, but we will keep our culture ahead of us.
>
> (The Winnipeg Art Gallery, *Cape Dorset*, p. 34)

In Kananginak's total print production of about 120 works, however, illustrations of camp scenes, traditional activities, and legends are in a minority. Kananginak, the hunter, specializes in naturalistic portrayals of animals and birds, particularly the latter. His representations of arctic birds and animals are characterized by the accuracy and realism of wing and feather structure, colouring, shading, and texture. This is achieved by Kananginak even in monochrome engraving; for example, using strokes of different length and density, he has managed to convey the different colours and textures of the fur on a summer caribou in No. 43. And the black edition of the *Kupanuaq* print (No. 46) even without colour shows the shading on the body of the snow birds and conveys a sense of three-dimensionality. As Kananginak explains he has spent a lot of time observing the animals he now represents:

> When I became old enough to go around by myself, without my sister watching over me, I started hunting birds. I quietly studied their movements and grew to love them. Later I began to observe the varieties of birds that arrived in the arctic every spring. I studied the shapes, sizes, colours and sounds of different types of birds. . . . At that time I never knew that I was going to be drawing birds in the future.
>
> Animals are much more difficult to observe than birds. . . . Whenever I could, however, I enjoyed watching the powerful movements of the animals, and envied their gracefulness and intelligence.
>
> (1981 Cape Dorset print catalogue, p. 9)

One has only to compare Kananginak's birds with those of Kenojuak (Nos. 47-54), another Cape Dorset artist famous for her birds, to fully recognize Kananginak's naturalism. Kananginak birds have an entirely different character; they are birds closely seen and carefully drawn by a hunter. Kenojuak's birds, on the other hand, are only the starting point for elaborate, dense, flat, and almost abstract designs. Kananginak's actual drawing technique is also different from that of Kenojuak who begins drawing without preliminary planning and whose colours add variety rather than realism to an already rich design. Kananginak explains his drawing technique:

> I can never start drawing unless I have something in my head. Only when I can really clearly see the picture in my head, then I start drawing. I can't ever draw when I don't have it really worked out in my head. I don't really like drawings too colourful. The thing I really like is when the colours are matching or when they're almost the same — when the colours are like real.
>
> (1978 Cape Dorset print catalogue, p. 46)

42.
Kananginak (1935–) m.
Caribou Hunt 1964
Engraving 26/50
30.6 x 45.2 cm
78/309

43.
Kananginak (1935–) m.
Summer Caribou 1973
Engraving 42/50
31.5 x 45.5 cm
78/507

44.
Kananginak (1935–) m.
Printed by Lukta (1928–) m.
Owl of Kingait 1973
Stonecut 22/50
70.4 x 62.3 cm
78/511

45.
Kananginak (1935–) m.
Printed by Saggiaktok (1943–) m.
Kupanuaq 1975
Stonecut 16/50
61.0 x 85.0 cm
78/358

Note:
The same image was printed in two
editions; No. 46 in black, No. 45 in colour.

46. (Not Illustrated)
Kananginak (1935–) m.
Printed by Saggiaktok (1943–) m.
Kupanuaq 1975
Stonecut 40/50
61.0 x 84.7 cm
78/361

In much of Kenojuak's early work the flatness, emphasis on positive/ negative space, and interconnecting images are reminiscent of her techniques as a seamstress. In fact, the first Kenojuak print published, *Rabbit Eating Seaweed* (1959/8), was taken directly from the design on a sealskin bag made by the artist. The seamstresses of south Baffin, in making their highly decorated traditional garments, used different coloured skins to create contrasting inset designs. Kenojuak's early graphics, such as *Dream* (No. 48), have characteristics in common with this sewing technique, with its concern for outline, interrelationship, contrast, and the way individual elements are distributed over a larger surface, often repeated or mirrored along a central vertical axis.

Many of these techniques continue to be used over the years, but Kenojuak is continually expanding on them and experimenting with new ways of embellishing her images. According to Kenojuak, the actual subject matter of her drawings is less important than what she does with it; the subject functions as a means to an end.

> For my subject matter I don't start off and pick a subject as such; that's not my way of addressing a drawing. My way of doing it is to start without a preconceived plan of exactly what I am going to execute in full, and so I come up with a small part of it which is pleasing to me and I use that as a starting point to wander into, through the drawing. I may start off at one end of a form not even knowing what the entirety of the form is going to be; just drawing as I am thinking, thinking as I am drawing. . . . And rather what I do is I try to make things which satisfy my eye, which satisfy my sense of form and colour. It's more an interplay of form and colour which I enjoy performing and I do it until it satisfies my eye and then I am on to something else.
>
> (personal interview, May, 1980)

That birds should be such a popular subject in Kenojuak's drawings has no particular significance; she explains simply that she likes birds and that when she starts to draw they are often what emerge on the paper. Certainly too, birds, unlike narrative or realistic scenes, lend themselves to her style of drawing with its emphasis on graphic elaboration rather than straightforward representation. Rarely are Kenojuak's birds done with the simplicity so effectively achieved in the *Two Ravens* (No. 49). Even in the early drawings, the birds do not remain unembellished; wings and feathers are elongated and sweep off the bird's body in elegant swirls and delicate fans.

Over the years the elaboration of the bird image becomes more and more complex; Kenojuak extends the feather structure and adds in decorative motifs such as foliage or other birds which become denser and denser until they overlap, superimpose, and crowd each other. In addition, these motifs are further embellished with different kinds of dots and linear markings similar to those used over the surface of a bird to show the different feathers on various parts of his body. Colour is also used to enrich the image. As with Kenojuak's other techniques, her use of colour is the result of careful esthetic consideration; as she explains, she puts out the colours she is going to use ahead of time, pairing up those she wishes to use together and deciding what combinations are the most pleasing to her.

With all these embellishments and additions the bird subject is increasingly affected and by the early 1970s the bird form itself had virtually succumbed to its decoration. In the 1970 drawing *Owl* (No. 53), the bird is recognizable only by its eyes; even the nose is a decorative shape, and the body, which originally played a major role in the process of beautification, has all but disappeared. Kenojuak never reaches the point of complete abstraction in her images, but drawings such as this one illustrate how her esthetic concerns have completely overridden the subject matter. This approach is contrary to that of more realistic artists such as Kananginak who, as hunters, are more interested in creating a real and true image of the animal or bird.

By the early to mid-1970s Kenojuak seems to have pushed the bird subject as far as possible without completely abstracting it, and she turned to other subjects such as the human face while approaching the bird subject from another angle. The bird itself is reinstated in basic bird form; much of the decoration takes place within the bird-like outline and more attention is given to surface definition and colourful embellishments that do not alter the shape so much as add to it.

There is little action or narration in Kenojuak's work, nor are there many depictions of legendary, mythological, or everyday activities. Her concern continues to be with what the image looks like, not with what is represented; as she says, she is just trying to "make something beautiful, that's all" (Blodgett, *Kenojuak*, p. 41).

47.
Kenojuak (1927–) f.
Printed by Iyola (1933–) m.
Sun Owl 1963
Stonecut 30/50
61.7 x 92.2 cm
78/286

48.
Kenojuak (1927–) f.
Printed by Lukta (1928–) m.
Dream 1963
Stonecut 32/50
71.0 x 62.3 cm
78/287

49.
Kenojuak (1927–) f.
Printed by Iyola (1933–) m.
Two Ravens 1968
Stencil 30/50
50.5 x 63.4 cm
78/339

50.
Kenojuak (1927–) f.
Printed by Lukta (1928–) m.
Night Hunter 1969
Stonecut 7/50
61.8 x 83.5 cm
78/334

51.
Kenojuak (1927–) f.
Printed by Lukta (1928–) m.
Birds and Foliage 1970
Stonecut 35/50
61.8 x 87.0 cm
78/485

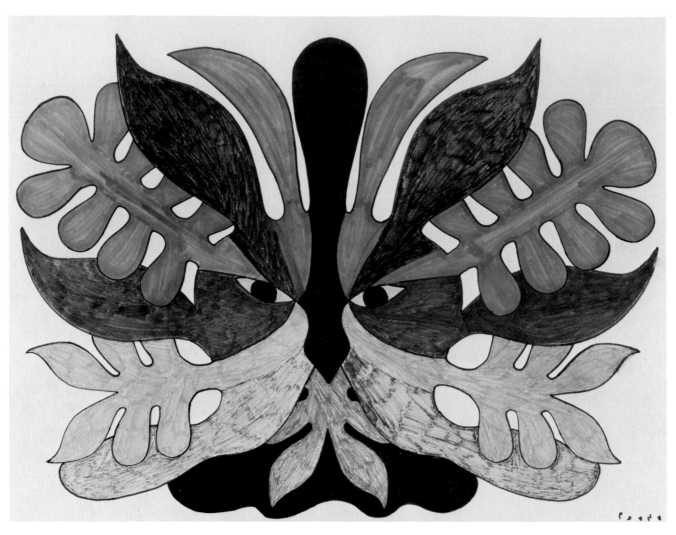

53.
Kenojuak (1927–) f.
Owl 1970
Felt-tip pen
50.8 x 66.0 cm
Signed lower right with syllabics; dated
   on verso by Cooperative
78/549

52.
Kenojuak (1927–) f.
Bird with Colourful Plumage 1970
Felt-tip pen
50.7 x 66.3 cm
Signed lower right with syllabics; dated
   on verso by Cooperative
78/176
See colour plate on page 26.

54.
Kenojuak (1927–) f.
Printed by Saggiaktok (1943–) m.
Young Girl's Thoughts of Birds 1974
Stonecut 47/50
61.8 x 85.7 cm
78/355

KIAKSHUK

Fig. 11.
Kiakshuk (1886-1966) m.
Printed by Iyola (1933–) m.
Cape Dorset
Three Bear Hunters 1960
Stencil
51.2 x 64.4 cm

Fig. 12.
Kiakshuk (1886-1966) m.
Printed by Lukta (1928–) m.
Cape Dorset
Baffin Woman 1960
Stonecut
72.8 x 54.2 cm
National Museum of Man,
   National Museums of Canada
   Neg. No. 80-9706

Kiakshuk was born in Arctic Quebec, but sometime around the turn of the century his family migrated across the Hudson Straits to southwest Baffin Island. Their trip, done partly by *umiak* (large skin-covered boat), partly aboard the *Active*, was a combination of the traditional and the new, typical of the changing times. But Kiakshuk was born of a generation that still knew and practised the old ways. He himself lived in camps in the area between Cape Dorset and Andrew Gordon Bay until late in his life when he settled permanently in Cape Dorset to live with his son, the well-known printer Lukta. Kiakshuk was in his seventies when he began drawing for the Co-op, and his graphic work reflects the traditional Inuit values, beliefs, and practices which he knew so well.

Living on the land as he did, Kiakshuk's life was oriented to the hunt, and many of his works illustrate this preoccupation. There are scenes of animals in which Kiakshuk unites and intertwines a wide range of different animals as though suggesting their universal relationship and interdependence. In the graphics with both people and animals, the human beings do not dominate the scene; instead, they are only another component, equal in importance and size to their fellow animals, as though recognizing that, even with certain superior characteristics, man is still dependent on products from the animal world for food, clothing, light, and warmth. Man's dependent and tenuous position in this world is, in fact, emphasized – not without humour – in some of Kiakshuk's works. Small men in boats seem lost and forlorn among a large gathering of animals (No. 58) while in the print *Three Bear Hunters* (fig. 11) a ferocious, prickly bear so worries his three human opponents that one flees in terror.

Some of Kiakshuk's graphics such as *Eskimo Wrestling Two Spirits* (No. 55) and *Strange Scene* (1964-65/21) are truly strange, even terrifying. Looking at Kiakshuk's scenes one is reminded of the words of the Igloolik shaman Aua recorded by Knud Rasmussen in the early 1920s: "We do not believe, we fear" (*Iglulik Eskimos*, p. 54). The comparison with Aua here is doubly appropriate since Kiakshuk was not only regarded as a great hunter, he was also recognized as a shaman. Fear was a constant companion for the lonely, beleaguered hunter who had to contend with the real dangers of this world – with attacking bears, rapidly changing weather conditions, or starving and maddened humans – and with the even more terrifying dangers of the world of the supernatural – the evil spirits, the powerful sea goddess and the souls of the dead. Shamans, such as Kiakshuk, knew only too well the omnipotent and omnipresent character of other-worldly beings and spirits.

Yet these things cannot be helped. Life still goes on, and Kiakshuk also shows us typical scenes of everyday life: singing women sew a kayak (1960/29), people go about in a busy summer camp (No. 57), and men load fur bales (1966/34). Rarely are we simply shown human beings as in the 1960 drawing of *Seated Figures* (No. 56) included here. Dressed in the typically elaborate south Baffin parkas with inset contrasting decoration, two rows of figures sit on little stools. The repetition of forms and the alternating male and female figures create a sense of rhythm in this finely and gently delineated drawing. The female figure in the lower right is somewhat similar to that in a Kiakshuk print entitled *Baffin Woman* (fig. 12) done the same year, but not reproduced in the annual print catalogue.

55.
Kiakshuk (1886-1966) m.
Printed by Kananginak (1935–) m.
Eskimo Wrestling Two Spirits 1960
Stencil 2/50
45.3 x 57.0 cm
78/249

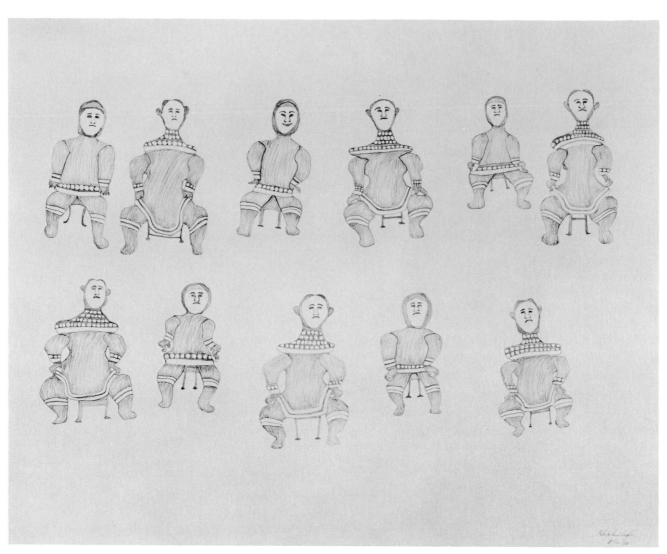

56.
Kiakshuk (1886-1966) m.
Seated Figures 1960
Graphite
47.9 x 59.3 cm
Signed and dated lower right by
    Cooperative
78/665

57.
Kiakshuk (1886-1966) m.
Printed by Lukta (1928–) m.
Summer Camp Scene 1961
Stencil 26/50
60.5 x 73.8 cm
78/251

58.
Kiakshuk (1886-1966) m.
Untitled 1962
Engraving 45/50
33.2 x 48.7 cm
78/269

KINGMEATA ETIDLOOIE

In the 1978 Cape Dorset print catalogue (p. 55) Kingmeata states: "I enjoy using the acrylic paints more than ordinary pencils and paper. I find painting easier than drawing and I like the way the finished picture looks better." Her painterly talents were first recognized, when Kingmeata was still using pencils and felt-tip pens, by Terry Ryan who made an effort to see that she was provided with watercolours. Singled out as she was, Kingmeata began painting in the early 1970s and has worked extensively in acrylics since then.

Acrylic painting, which a number of Cape Dorset artists have tried since the mid-seventies, is generally undertaken in a studio space provided by the Cooperative. While drawing with pencil is usually done at home (although a drawing studio has just recently been set up in Dorset), most people find acrylic paints too messy to use in the cramped, child-filled spaces of their homes. In Cape Dorset, acrylics are characteristically mixed to a thin wash much like watercolour and are applied to paper not canvas.

Both in her drawing and painting Kingmeata concentrates on fairly simple compositions. The early prints sometimes show an elaboration of a few motifs with complex swirls and extensions, while drawings such as the *Six Birds* (No. 59) illustrate her enriching use of colour, here applied in sensitive pointillistic dots. In her drawings Kingmeata consciously restricts the complexity of her image in contrast to works by her husband Etidlooie which, with their small and numerous subjects, she considers very complicated for the printers to have to make into prints. But as she also points out, her poor eyesight is an additional factor in their different approaches.

Kingmeata's subjects range from birds, people, and animals to a wide variety of composite and transformed creatures. In a print such as *Dog Dreams of Seal* (No. 60) we are shown a thought in visual terms, a technique used in other Cape Dorset graphics like the Pitseolak *Dream of Motherhood* (No. 88), but in Kingmeata's work in general the image does not tell a story or depict a specific event. Popular subjects such as the bird may appear in a straightforward representation, or as the basis for an elaborated design, or as one of several compositional elements in a conglomerate design.

Kingmeata's technical concerns and abilities as a colourist, along with her imagination, find expression in acrylic paintings such as *Scene* (No. 61). In this work we see characteristics typical of her painting: the unusual but successful mix of colours; the wild creature, bird, and human subjects; a general landscape setting for these subjects rather than a detailed or specific place; and the unidentifiable motifs that function as elements in the design such as the *inukshuk*-like object on top of one of the hills.

59.
Kingmeata (1915–) f.
Six Birds c. 1969
Felt-tip pen and graphite
50.7 x 66.5 cm
Signed lower right with syllabics
78/547
See colour plate on page 20.

60.
Kingmeata (1915–) f.
Printed by Saggiaktok (1943–) m.
Dog Dreams of Seal 1973
Stonecut 31/50
43.1 x 62.8 cm
78/645

61.
Kingmeata (1915–) f.
Scene 1976
Acrylic
47.0 x 58.8 cm
Signed lower right with syllabics; dated
  on verso by Cooperative
78/184

Perhaps even more disconcerting to the uninitiated viewer of Inuit art than the weird transformed spirit creatures are those depictions that show otherwise ordinary animals in abnormal poses. Bears dance, birds recline, and walruses sit upright. In a culture that traditionally believed in spirits and transformation, including the ability of humans to change into animals and animals into humans, such occurrences are not unusual or even remarkable. These beliefs are still reflected in art works from throughout the north, especially in carvings from Cape Dorset where the artists continually test and expand the limitations of their subject matter, the sculptural form, and even the limits of their sculptural medium.

Such concerns characterize the work of Kiugak who began to carve in 1947 before the establishment of an arts and crafts program at Cape Dorset. As he says, "I started to carve by myself. I had the talent for carving. When I start[ed] carving, I was good at carving already . . . I was one of the first ones to carve" (interview with Marion Jackson, February, 1979). The son of Pitseolak the graphic artist (Nos. 84-93), Kiugak has done some graphic work himself – one of his stonecuts was published in the 1960 collection, one stonecut and two engravings in 1963 – but it is as a sculptor that Kiugak is primarily known. He has had a long and productive career; his biographical sheet compiled by the Department of Indian and Northern Affairs lists more than thirty group exhibitions and two one-man shows.

Kiugak's sculptural career has been fairly well documented and published illustrations from various sources give a suggestive but incomplete picture of his changing concerns and techniques. For example, the human figure, which is a popular subject in his work, is presented in a typical 1950s three-dimensional representational style in his 1954 sculpture of a mother and child (Watt, *Canadian Guild of Crafts Quebec*, No. 152). In his works from the late 1970s and early 1980s (Agnes Etherington Art Centre, *Inuit Art in the 1970's*, No. 45), Kiugak tends to flatten and open up his sculptures, emphasizing the spaces between interconnecting, curving human and animal forms.

In contrast to this flamboyant, elaborate presentation of representational and everyday subjects, works from the late fifties and sixties, such as the walrus illustrated on the opposite page, show a greater interest in unusual subjects sometimes shown in innovative poses. Although some of these poses are unusual, the presentation at this time is more restrained than the 1970s pieces, the sculptural elements more tightly contained within the basic form. Kiugak's unusual subjects during this time resulted in carvings of dancing sea creatures, a growling lion rearing up on his hind legs, a howling *tornrak* (spirit) with its young, and seated and standing walruses, one carrying an incised tusk on his shoulder. The latter walrus (The Winnipeg Art Gallery, *Cape Dorset*, No. 10), although somewhat subordinated to the tusk it carries, is comparable in pose and in such details as flippers, eyes, whiskers, and tusks to the one illustrated here. In both sculptures, which incidentally date from the same year, the walrus is balanced in an unnatural position, the flippers equalizing and supporting the animal's weight.

62.
Kiugak Ashoona (1933–) m.
Walrus Spirit c. 1962
Green/black stone and ivory
30.0 x 18.2 x 31.5 cm
Unsigned
78/432

KOVINAKTILLIAK PARR

Of the nineteen prints by Kovinaktilliak Parr – the son of Parr (Nos. 74-79) and Eleeshushe (No. 33) – published between 1961 and 1976, all but one, a stonecut, have been engravings. Generally portraying people, camp and hunting scenes, or animal compositions, Kovinaktilliak has concentrated on his engraving technique. In a number of prints, such as the one illustrated here (No. 63), the subject is kept fairly simple with a stable interlocking compositional format, but the motifs are quite elaborately detailed with different types of markings and patterns.

In our print the bulky, happy hunter stands astride two walruses, whom he obviously has the better of. The walruses' eyes and ivory tusks have been left white, while their whiskers are delineated with long thin parallel lines and their hide with quick short dashes – the type of marking also used to show the texture of the hide used in the man's sealskin clothing. The man's own hair and his fur collar are distinguished from other types of engraved lines, while the de-haired skin soles of his *kamiks* and the contrasting decorations on his parka have been left white.

63.
Kovinaktilliak Parr (1930-) m.
Happy Hunter 1974
Engraving 40/50
45.5 X 31.8 cm
78/349

LACHAULASSIE AKESUK

Concentrating on a limited number of subjects, and using only a few kinds of markings or surface definition, Lachaulassie creates a wide range of animal/human creatures in a variety of poses. The two most popular subjects in Lachaulassie's work are the sea goddess and the bird. While the former retains her basic characteristics with some variation in size or pose, the birds squat, recline, and grow unbirdlike appendages; they become part-human or impossibly tall and fat.

In contrast to the depictions of birds by other artists in the community such as Kananginak's naturalistic birds, Kenojuak's elaborately decorated birds, Lucy's friendly ever-present birds, Shiuqyuk's fragile birds, or Osuitok's strange bird spirits, in fact, birds of all kinds of elaborate visual forms, Lachaulassie's birds are stark and minimal, a style reminiscent of his late father Tudlik's.

Yet an examination of Lachaulassie birds demonstrates his ability to be very expressive within his limited repertoire. It would not be sufficient to say that the birds each look different one from another; they also have different qualities, as though each was an individual being, animated by a distinct character. There are self-important birds, skittish birds, happy birds, lazy birds, elegant birds, human birds, and stodgy birds. And all this is achieved with such a limited amount of reworking of the stone.

Lachaulassie and Solomonie Tigullaraq of Clyde River (No. 105) are brothers.

64.
Lachaulassie Akesuk (1919-) m.
Reclining Bird c. 1968
Green/black stone
23.5 x 42.2 x 17.8 cm
Unsigned
78/678

65.
Lachaulassie Akesuk (1919-   ) m.
Owl c. 1968
Grey stone
32.5 x 24.0 x 23.3 cm
Unsigned
78/221

LUCY QUINNUAJUAK

Many of Lucy's graphics are alive with her distinctive wide-eyed birds; there are colourful, acrobatic, spectator, nesting, courting, and strutting birds. The birds eat, play, meet and dance; they try to wrestle fish from a fisherwoman; they perch on people's hands; they fly overhead; and they get caught in tents. In the graphite drawing (No. 66), a large flock of birds gather together, standing on rocks and on each other, and even growing from one another.

This drawing is of particular interest because it is the original for the 1963 Lucy print *Family of Birds* (fig. 13). A comparison of the two points out the difference between the original drawing, with its erasures and reworkings as in the mid-left, and the finished print, illustrating the changes that can take place in the printing process. Starting from an outline tracing, the stonecutter may change markings, colours, and other details to clarify or simplify the image as he sees fit. In the drawing Lucy has used different markings to distinguish the various types of birds and to add variety. There are short hatch marks, U-shaped and circular markings, curved parallel lines, as well as areas that are filled in with light or dark application of graphite and that are in contrast to those areas that are left white.

Lucy did not carve, and there are only two engravings by her in the annual print collections, but she has done many drawings from which to date about 115 prints have been published since 1961. There is much that is whimsical and lighthearted in Lucy's graphics, from the ruffled, inquisitive, cute, and ponderous bird characters in this drawing (No. 66) to the juxtaposition of the feeding bird in the upper left of *Scene* (No. 68) who dwarfs the human being next to him. Rarely concerned with legendary or spiritual themes, Lucy tended to concentrate on everyday subjects such as birds and human beings – like those in *Joyful Mothers* (1971/33) – that are relevant and dear to the Inuit woman. These motifs, nevertheless, are presented by Lucy in imaginative formats and combinations.

Fig. 13.
Lucy (1915-1982) f.
Printed by Lukta (1928-) m.
Cape Dorset
Family of Birds 1963
Stonecut
61.8 x 87.0 cm
National Museum of Man,
    National Museums of Canada
    Neg. No. 82-8573

66.
Lucy (1915-1982) f.
Family of Birds 1962
Graphite drawing for 1963 print (1963/66)
46.0 x 61.2 cm
Signed and dated on verso by Cooperative
78/563

68.
Lucy (1915-1982) f.
Scene 1977
Coloured pencil and acrylic
56.0 x 75.8 cm
Signed lower right with syllabics; dated
   on verso by Cooperative
78/669
See colour plate on page 24.

67.
Lucy (1915-1982) f.
Printed by Ottochie (1904-1982) m.
Tulukara 1977
Stonecut and stencil 38/50
58.9 x 63.0 cm
78/369

NATSIVAAR

Only two prints by Natsivaar have been published in the annual Cape Dorset collections; this one (No. 69) in 1960, another in 1961. The 1961 print entitled *Mother and Son* (1961/59) shows a male figure, a dog, and a woman with an *ulu* in her hand and a child in her *amautiq*. The subject matter, the disproportionate size of the figures, and the style of clothing with its contrasting inset decoration can all be said to be typical of early Cape Dorset graphics.

Not so with Natsivaar's other print *Angels in the Moon* (No. 69). Here two strange creatures float near a fairy-tale moon. The Christian subject matter, the non-Inuit facial shapes and beards of the angels, and the way the moon is depicted all point to Western sources. Certainly by the time this work was done the south Baffin Inuit had been converted to Christianity or at least been well exposed to Western religious concepts and literature as well as secular sources. These new ideas were often as well integrated into existing aspects of Inuit culture as Natsivaar's angels and moon are into Cape Dorset graphics. The angel, after all, is just a Western variant of the transformed creature and, while we have a man in the moon, in Inuit legends the moon was originally the brother of the woman who became the sun. There is nothing jarring or alien about Natsivaar's angels or moon in this haunting image from the Arctic.

69.
Natsivaar (1919-1962) f.
Printed by Iyola (1933-) m.
Angels in the Moon 1960
Stonecut 43/50
65.0 x 49.6 cm
78/248

In early 1951 when James and Alma Houston journeyed by dog team from Frobisher Bay to Cape Dorset, their requests for sculpture and crafts for export to the south were greeted with the information that the best carver on the south Baffin coast was Osuitok. First asked to carve in the 1940s by those at the Roman Catholic mission, Osuitok made small ivory models of such things as kayaks and fox traps; the latter completely functional on a miniature scale. As well, he fashioned incised scenes on ivory tusks or even musk-ox horn (Watt, *Canadian Guild of Crafts Quebec*, No. 49).

Writing for the *Cape Dorset* exhibition catalogue in 1980, the Houstons (see Introduction, p. 13) both recalled memories of their first meeting with the artist in 1951 (The Winnipeg Art Gallery, *Cape Dorset*, pp. 10, 14):

> Oshaweetok and his kindly wife Nepeesha had the neatest, most impressive igloo I had ever seen. It had canvas pinned to a light wooden inner frame completely covered with snow blocks. It was evenly warmed by a well tended seal oil lamp. Animal and bird drawings from Dewey Soper's books had been carefully removed and pasted to the low ceiling so that one could lie in the Oshaweetok family's bed and carefully study them. I was so impressed by Oshaweetok and Nepeesha and his ivory carving then in progress and the warm hospitality of his compact family dwelling.
>
> (James Houston)

> At last, we reached Itiliakjuk and there he was, a thin, handsome man with a sudden, shy smile and beautiful, sensitive hands. His snowhouse was sparkling, dry, its interior walls papered with fresh looking pages from newspapers and magazines. We talked about our project; Osoetuk was quick in his enthusiasm. Caring greatly about his language and cultural heritage and, like his neighbours, experiencing hardship in gaining a living, he saw at once the possibilities inherent in the plan. He would help us.
>
> (Alma Houston)

It was Osuitok's association with the Houstons that led to the first printmaking experiments in Cape Dorset. Responding to Osuitok's comments about how tedious it must be for someone to paint continually the identical images such as he saw on two cigarette packages, Houston demonstrated basic image transfer using one of Osuitok's own incised ivory scenes, ink, and toilet paper. Osuitok, Houston, and other men collaborated in making the early prints, and there were two Osuitok prints in the 1957/58 group of graphics and another two in the 1959 collection. (Although those from 1957/58 were the first body of prints released in the south, they were uncatalogued and are still poorly documented; those from 1959 were the first collection from Cape Dorset that was officially catalogued.) Osuitok did not continue to work in the printshop, however, and since his prints *Four Muskoxen* and *Owl, Fox and Hare Legend* of 1959, there have been no other graphics by him in the annual collections.

Clearly Osuitok's interest and certainly his talents lie in the field of carving. The five Osuitok sculptures included in the Masterworks exhibition (Canadian Eskimo Arts Council, *Sculpture/Inuit*, Nos. 143, 165, 166, 168, 190) demonstrate his sculptural finesse, his delicate detailing and inset work, his fine finishing, and his penchant for an impossibly balanced mass. Several of the sculptures show birds – their whole body in some cases dangerously cantilevered – finely balanced on both legs or

72.
Osuitok Ipeelee (1923-) m.
Caribou Head c. 1970
Green stone and antler
54.7 X 31.5 X 45.6 cm
Signed with syllabics
78/244
See colour plate on page 19.

71.
Osuitok Ipeelee (1923-) m.
Bear Spirit c. 1969
Green stone
40.5 X 31.4 X 10.5 cm
Signed with syllabics
78/197

70A

70.
Osuitok Ipeelee (1923-) m.
Bird Spirit c. 1968
Green stone
33.5 x 35.8 x 12.9 cm
Signed with syllabics
78/685

even just one of them. The works are not only physically balanced on one fine point but they are compositionally balanced so that there is no feeling of awkward top-heaviness.

Osuitok, the brother of two other well-known Cape Dorset carvers Shiuqyuk and Enooky, continues to achieve this sense of esthetic and physical balance in his carvings in such works as the stylized bear (No.

70B

71) and the elaborately horned caribou head (No. 72) where exaggeration is tempered with realism. Osuitok's carvings tend to be of animal and human subjects, although the former especially may be altered and changed as in *Bird Spirit* (No. 70) – the transformation and sculptural license working together to create images far more effective than just the representational.

OTTOCHIE TIMOTHY

Described by Terry Ryan (see Introduction, p. 13) in the 1979 Cape Dorset catalogue (p. 11) as "an ageless gentleman . . . to this day the most consistent and talented of the stone block cutters in spite of failing eyesight," Ottochie was recognized for his adroitness and patience in carving complex images into the stones for printing. The most time-consuming and difficult cutting jobs were regularly undertaken by this amiable, unhurried old hunter who worked at the printshop until his recent death. Ottochie joined the original group of printers in the early days of Cape Dorset printmaking. Not long after, in 1961, the printmakers, who had until then worked with stencil and stone block printing, began experimenting with copper-plate engraving.

In contrast to their other printing techniques in which they generally printed images derived from the drawings and designs of others, during the engraving experiments the printers both originated and printed their own images, as well as printing plates cut by others. Thus in the early 1960s, printers like Ottochie who became much better known in later years for printing other artists' work, also created images of their own making. Of the seven published Ottochie prints (all engravings), six date from the 1962 collection, one from 1963.

Ottochie, the other printers who tried engraving, and those artists who continue to do engraving all seem to work directly on the plate without benefit of preliminary drawings. Ottochie engravings such as the *Untitled* work illustrated here (No. 73) depict subjects relevant to a hunter and they have an air of immediacy and sketchiness, as basic as his early carvings of lumpish, chunky birds (Watt, *Canadian Guild of Crafts Quebec*, Nos. 27, 108). Evident in this engraving are small mistakes where the burin seems to have slipped or cut too far. Perhaps this is an early work, for in his 1963 engraving *Bear, Walrus and Duck* (1963/64) Ottochie's technique is much more assured and controlled, indicative of his tremendous cutting skills which would be responsible for the preparation of so many stone blocks over the next twenty years.

73.
Ottochie (1904-1982) m.
Untitled 1962
Engraving 34/50
24.6 x 33.2 cm
78/273

Parr, the old hunter, has given us immediate, basic, and direct records of life as he lived it. His creatures are not elaborately defined with markings or details, they are not even particularly well-proportioned, and sometimes one type of four-legged animal cannot be distinguished from another, yet we have no trouble in recognizing what is taking place or understanding what is important.

Many of Parr's works are concerned with the hunt, and as an aspect of this, with animals. His pieces of paper abound with caribou, walruses, birds, bears, seals, and dogs – individually, in herds, or all gathered together in unusual groupings without regard for perspective. While the hunter spears a dangerous bear, birds walk unconcernedly beneath its feet (No. 79). Nevertheless, we are left in no doubt as to the importance and ferociousness of the bear; this is indicated not only by its bared teeth, but also by its large size in proportion to the man and the other animals. The caribou in the drawing *Seven Caribou* (No. 78) look not unlike this bear, yet their antlers do distinguish them. And somehow what exact type of animal they really are seems secondary to the visual image in which the different shapes and sizes are so effectively distributed and repeated with the accent of red horns.

Although there are scenes of successful hunters bringing home their catch, or scenes with captured prey as in *Day's End* (No. 76), the overall impression remains that far too often the hunter is in continual pursuit of his prey. He appears as the human figure off to one side in a scene full of animals, sometimes with weapon in hand, sometimes united to an animal by a length of harpoon line. In these scenes it is not so much that game is not available – there always seem to be lots of animals – it is just that they are so elusive and hard to catch.

People are the other important subject in Parr's drawings – the hunters who pursue their game, the groups of Inuit as in *My People* (No. 74), or the family snug in their dwelling at *Day's End* (No. 76). No matter that their faces are hidden by parka hoods or indicated with just a few little parallel lines and that their bodies are of the strangest shapes, we sense the relations and companionship.

Parr first began drawing in early 1961 at the request of Terry Ryan (see Introduction, page 13) who later wrote, "From the very first, he was obviously intrigued and totally committed to the undertaking, for he drew on both sides of the sheets, completely filling the very sizable area" (West Baffin Eskimo Cooperative, *Parr*, p. 4). Although he did do some engraving, Parr preferred drawing and he continued to draw prolifically and continually until his death eight years later. Parr's work is readily identifiable, with its characteristic style – linear, exaggerated and disproportionate – a style that went unappreciated by a number of his fellow Cape Dorset artists. Parr signed many of his drawings, with pride and humour, his one-syllable name signified by the syllabic letter < which appears in some unexpected places in his compositions as in the upper right in *Seven Caribou* (No. 78), between the man and bear in *Bear Hunt* (No. 79) and – could it be? – in an outlined area at the mid-right of the dwelling in *Day's End* (No. 76).

75.
Parr (1893-1969) m.
Walrus Hunters with Dog Sled 1961
Graphite
47.7 x 60.6 cm
Dated on verso by Cooperative
78/554

76.
Parr (1893-1969) m.
Printed by Iyola (1933-) m.
Day's End 1962
Stonecut 34/50
50.0 x 62.7 cm
78/255

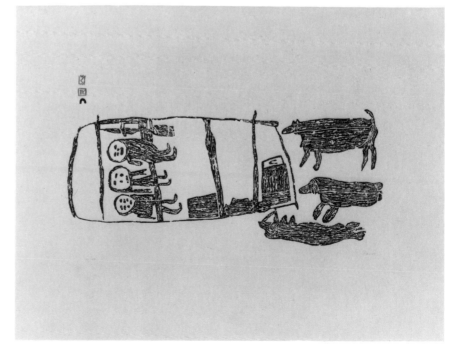

74. Opposite
Parr (1893-1969) m.
Printed by Lukta (1928-) m.
My People 1961
Stonecut 50/50
76.4 x 50.8 cm
78/252

79.
Parr (1893-1969) m.
Bear Hunt 1966
Felt-tip pen
50.8 x 65.6 cm
Signed lower mid-right with syllabics;
    dated on verso by Cooperative
78/550

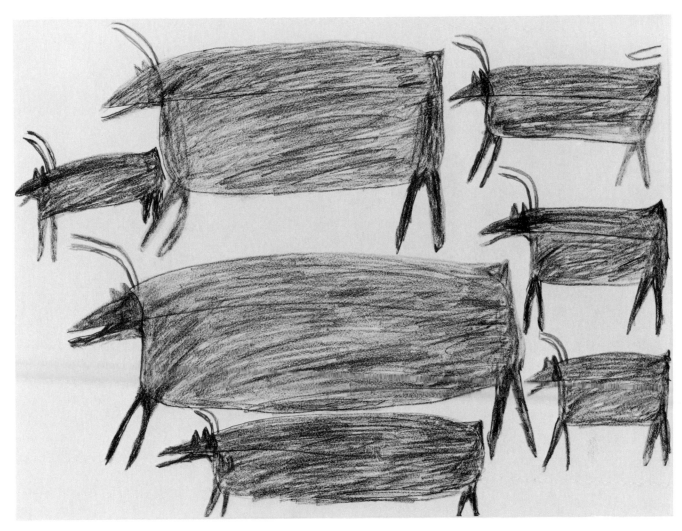

78.
Parr (1893-1969) m.
Seven Caribou 1964
Wax crayon
50.8 x 65.8 cm
Signed upper right with syllabics; dated
   on verso by Cooperative
78/551
See colour plate on page 30.

77.
Parr (1893-1969) m.
Harpooning Walrus 1963
Engraving 22/50
31.2 x 40.5 cm
78/291

PAUTA SAILA

Many of Pauta's engravings such as the two included here (Nos. 80 and 81) differ quite considerably in style from his drawings (and the stonecuts and lithographs made from them). In contrast to the loose, rounded, basic shapes of the latter, the engravings are often done with a tightly controlled, delicate precision. Certainly the particular medium itself can influence an artist's style, although works by Parr, for example, whether drawn or engraved, are virtually the same. Using a metal burin to engrave into copper is physically difficult and artists like Kenojuak talk about how tiring it is and how she fears cutting herself. In Pauta's case, the pencil or felt-tip pen would have been a much easier means with which to achieve tiny precise details, yet it is the engravings not the drawings that are done in such painstaking, laborious detail. Nor can the difference between the two be attributed to a change in style over the years since engravings by Pauta in the 1968 collection are stylistically much closer to the 1962 to 1964 engravings than to contemporaneous drawings.

Pauta's engraving style is well illustrated by the 1963 *Owl* (No. 80) illustrated here. The body and wings of the bird are outlined with a dense wavy line, a continuous length with a multitude of up and down strokes, while the unfeathered legs and claws are outlined in a straighter heavier line. The suggestion of fuzzy feathers achieved with the wavy line is continued on the surface of the widely-spread wings which are covered with sequences of tiny zigzag strokes. The upper part of the wing on the right also has alternating rows of tiny dots. The lighter covering of body feathers are shown with groups of markings spaced over the surface. This feathery type of marking is used over the entire body surface of the other *Owl* (No. 81) illustrated here.

Of the approximately forty Pauta prints published between 1962 and 1981, many are devoted to one or two simple motifs, especially birds, bears, and human figures, often presented in single, frontal images like the 1963 *Owl*. Some of the later prints show vertical animal compositions, somewhat like totems. Usually there is little activity or movement in these prints; the participants either have no one to interact with or are balanced and fixed in place, like the elements in the drawing illustrated in fig. 14. Comparison of this drawing, compositionally very similar to his 1967 print *Walrus Totem* (1967/41), with the engravings points up the stylistic differences between Pauta's two graphic media – the irregular shape of the loosely drawn, minimally articulated bird, for example, in contrast to the symmetrical precision and varied markings of the engraved *Owl*.

Pauta, the husband of Pitaloosie (Nos. 82-83), is actually better known as a sculptor, recognized especially for his bears. These are often large in size but formally reduced to essential bear characteristics. He also carves other animals and birds, generally in a single or related subject format; for example, of his three works in the Masterworks exhibition there was a single bear, a bear family, and a musk-ox (Canadian Eskimo Arts Council, *Sculpture/Inuit*, Nos. 158, 122, 142). In 1967, Pauta took part in the International Sculpture Symposium in Toronto.

Fig. 14.
Pauta (1916-) m.
Cape Dorset
Composition c. 1967
Felt-tip pen
Art Gallery of Ontario
Gift of the Klamer Family, 1978

80.
Pauta (1916-) m.
Owl 1963
Engraving 21/50
31.4 x 45.0 cm
78/297

81.
Pauta (1916-) m.
Owl 1964
Engraving 50/50
31.4 x 45.3 cm
78/314

Birds, women, and mothers with their children are popular subjects in Pitaloosie's work, and here we have two variations on the feminine motif. In the print *Mother and Child* (No. 82) a delicate young woman with a child in her decorated *amautiq* is sewing a *kamik*. The child's head, large in proportion to that of the mother, slants out and away from the woman, but the thrust of the two heads leaning out at different angles is counterbalanced by the arch of the igloo wall around them. This curve of the schematic snow house effectively frames and unites the mother and child.

Although not particularly common in Pitaloosie's work, the mythological sea goddess Taleelayo is the subject of two 1974 prints and two of her drawings in the Klamer Collection. In the drawing included here (No. 83), the sea goddess is placed above a small seal in a pose reminiscent of certain sculptures which show the goddess riding a seal (fig. 15). This close association of the goddess and one of her sea animals effectively reinforces their relationship, and in Pitaloosie's drawing the seal visually supports the curving, swirling lines of Taleelayo's body. The felt-tip pen is used to add coloured details and markings and to define the heavy areas of the facial features and braid.

Pitaloosie spent many years of her youth in the Hamilton, Ontario hospital for tuberculosis patients. Once back in Cape Dorset she began doing drawings in the early 1960s for the Co-op. The first Pitaloosie prints were included in the 1968 Cape Dorset collection and there have been about sixty prints published since that time. Pitaloosie is married to the sculptor Pauta (Nos. 80-81).

Fig. 15.
Felix Kopak (1918-) m.
Repulse Bay
Sea Goddess Riding a Seal c. 1974
Grey-green stone
17.6 x 29.0 x 11.7 cm
Art Gallery of Ontario
Gift of the Klamer Family, 1978

83.
Pitaloosie (1942-) f.
Sea Goddess and Seal c. 1973
Felt-tip pen
51.2 x 65.8 cm
Signed lower right with syllabics
78/557

82.
Pitaloosie (1942-) f.
Printed by Iyola (1933-) m.
Mother and Child 1968
Stonecut 15/50
43.3 x 62.4 cm
78/336

Many Pitseolak works are imbued with a strong personal element illustrating actual people and events as she remembers them from her past. Some works such as the *Bear Attacking Seal* (No. 92) show more generalized scenes; others such as the engraving *Witch and Friends* (No. 85) depict subjects related to shamanism or other aspects of oral tradition. Most often the drawings reflect Pitseolak's own memories of her happy childhood and life on the land – travelling by *umiak*, snaring geese, playing *ayutaqtut*, sleeping in tents and igloos, and moving from camp to camp (in the summertime, harassed always by mosquitoes that in retrospect grow to tremendous size). Reading in the book *Pitseolak: Pictures Out of My Life*, her statement that she does not like insects comes as no surprise since she so graphically expresses this in her drawings. In our print *Summer Wanderers Watch Woman Scraping Hide* (No. 84) the women carry whisks to brush them off; in other graphics, giant mosquitoes attack from all directions.

Pitseolak's works are expressive of many emotions – the joys of motherhood, the desire to be a mother, the pleasure in sport, the excitement of pursuing game (meat to eat!), and the warm companionship of friends and family. In the drawing *Women Playing Ayutaqtut* (No. 90) she adds a written explanation of what is taking place, even identifying one person by name. The text on this drawing reads: "These women are playing *ayutaqtut*, a traditional game. They are playing this game with rope nets, swinging the ball inside the net and throwing it to another person. Here's Ashoona who throws the ball up in the air. The person in the lower left has just thrown the ball and the person in the upper centre is just about to catch it."

In these works Pitseolak reveals her own experiences and emotions to the extent that we feel we have some knowledge of her as a person. Certainly our knowledge of her is augmented by her reminiscences and comments in the biography edited by Dorothy Eber, but even so the art works are unusually revealing. Unlike many other Inuit artists who remove themselves from their work by representing typical but generalized scenes, by avoiding personal or social comments, or by their concentration on esthetic rather than narrative concerns, Pitseolak shows us her own life, as well as her personality, and even her drawings within drawings.

Two drawings in the Klamer Collection (No. 87 and fig. 16) have been identified by the artist as Pitseolak drawings of Pitseolak drawings. These works in which Pitseolak includes drawings of her drawings are of particular interest; representations such as Kenojuak's drawing showing herself at work on a drawing (unpublished), and Samisa's carving titled *Making a Carving* (Norman Mackenzie Art Gallery, *Schumiatcher Collection*, No. 119) are rare in Inuit art. Pitseolak's play on the idea of drawings within drawings gives us a fascinating insight into her thoughts and art making. In No. 87 and fig. 16 the drawings in the drawing are placed in outline frames and set apart from the animal and bird figures below them. In No. 87 the drawings are actually held up for display by four human figures, while in the other, the drawings within the drawing are simply placed in the upper part of the paper. The scenes depicted in the drawing drawings are, needless to say, done in a typical Pitseolak style.

More concerned with recording and portraying events than with esthetics, realism, or other formal aspects of art, Pitseolak tends to depict her subjects in a style less restrained and less precise than some of her peers. The rather strange, vague figures and the marvelously misshapen little dog in *Summer Wanderers Watch Woman Scraping Hide* (No. 84) have an awkwardness attributable to the early date of the work. This changes over the years as Pitseolak becomes more accomplished, although in prints such as the 1969 graphic titled *Legend of the Narwhal[e]*, several figures are still ill-proportioned. Many works, though, such as *Bear Attacking Seal* (No. 92) show ingenious and effective solutions to rendering three dimensions into two.

Pitseolak is a tremendously prolific artist who has done, as she herself has calculated, thousands of drawings. A number of these have been made into stonecut, stencil, and lithograph prints, and these along with the prints made from her engravings total a production of over 200 prints released between 1960 and 1981. During that time she has achieved considerable recognition and a number of honours; she is a member of the Royal Canadian Academy and has received a Canada Council senior arts grant and the Order of Canada. Pitseolak has been featured in several major solo exhibitions and her biography *Pitseolak: Pictures Out of My Life* was published in 1971. It is only appropriate to conclude with her much quoted statement from that book:

I am going to keep on doing them [drawings] until they tell me to stop. If no one tells me to stop, I shall make them as long as I am well. If I can, I'll make them even after I am dead.

Fig. 16.
Pitseolak (1904-) f.
Cape Dorset
Pitseolak Drawings in a Drawing 1968
Coloured pencil and felt-tip pen
50.8 x 65.6 cm
Art Gallery of Ontario
Gift of the Klamer Family, 1978

84.
Pitseolak (1904-) f.
Printed by Iyola (1933-) m.
Summer Wanderers Watch Woman
    Scraping Hide 1961
Stonecut 38/50
46.0 x 61.5 cm
78/136

85.
Pitseolak (1904-) f.
Witch and Friends 1963
Engraving 31/50
31.4 x 45.5 cm
78/300

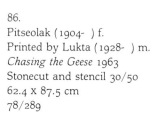

87.
Pitseolak (1904-) f
A Pitseolak Drawing of People Holding
  Pitseolak Drawings 1964
Graphite
50.7 x 65.2 cm
Signed lower centre right with syllabics;
  dated on verso by Cooperative
78/658

86.
Pitseolak (1904-) f.
Printed by Lukta (1928-) m.
Chasing the Geese 1963
Stonecut and stencil 30/50
62.4 x 87.5 cm
78/289

89.
Pitseolak (1904-) f.
Our Home 1969
Felt-tip pen
45.7 x 61.2 cm
Signed lower centre with syllabics; dated
    on verso by Cooperative
78/174

88.
Pitseolak (1904-) f.
Printed by Eegyvudluk (1931-) m.
Dream of Motherhood 1969
Stonecut 32/50
62.0 x 86.9 cm
78/141

90.
Pitseolak (1904·) f.
Women Playing Ayutaqtut 1969
Felt-tip pen
45.7 x 61.0 cm
Signed lower left centre with syllabics;
    dated on verso by Cooperative
78/660

91.
Pitseolak (1904-) f.
Printed by Ottochie (1904-1982) m.
Summer Voyage 1971
Stonecut 40/50
61.4 x 86.4 cm
78/489

93.
Pitseolak (1904-) f.
Printed by Saggiaktok (1943-) m.
Our Camp 1974
Stonecut 37/50
85.9 x 62.3 cm
78/353

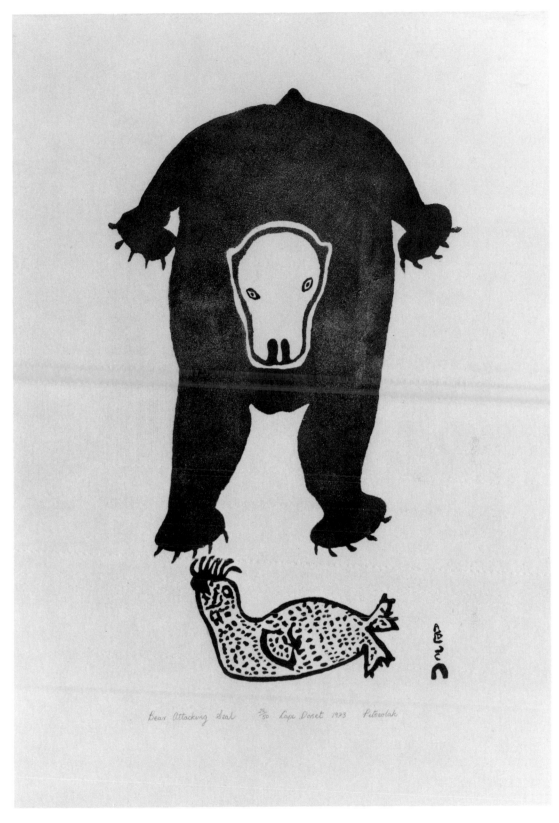

Bear Attacking Seal 22/50 Cape Dorset 1973 Pitseolak

92.
Pitseolak (1904-) f.
Printed by Lukta (1928-) m.
Bear Attacking Seal 1973
Stonecut 22/50
63.1 x 43.5 cm
78/521

Unlike many of his fellow artists who are such firm traditionalists, Pudlo represents a variety of non-traditional, non-Inuit subjects in his work. And unlike those artists who may occasionally represent such non-traditional things as snowmobiles and helicopters or themes derived from Christianity, Pudlo, especially in recent years, has made extensive use of these imported subjects.

These things may have been imported at one time, but they are now – and have been for some years – an integral part of life in the north, where snowmobiles far outnumber dog teams, where wooden boats have long replaced *umiaks*, where shamanism has been all but replaced by Christianity, where local radio phone-in talk shows have become forums for discussion, where plane travel is the norm, and where telephones and television sets bring the south that much closer. Far from being exotic, Pudlo's airplanes, helicopters, angels, and churches are part of northern reality. Instead it is the depictions of the old ways that are becoming an anomaly, and it appears that these depictions of traditional activities and scenes are inspired as much by nostalgia and a desire to preserve and document the old ways on the part of the artists as by the pressures exerted on the market by the romanticism of the southern buyer.

While Pudlo's recent graphics of airplanes are seen by some as "un-Eskimo," Pudlo has for years incorporated western elements into his work. Like shamans, spirits, or arctic animals, they are part of his Panofskyan "cultural equipment" and as such they are raw material for his creativity. Looking at the collection of Pudlo drawings in the archives of the West Baffin Eskimo Cooperative, one can see how Pudlo will take an image or concept and work with it, experimenting and searching for a visual solution. Western subjects are just as prone to this process as indigenous ones – fish become planes, birds become boats, telephone lines become necklaces, caribou become tents, and a door lock becomes a human-like figure holding a door handle and key.

The visual transformation of these subjects is all part of Pudlo's working process in which the drawing of one thing leads to another; sometimes subjects are repeated in new ways, other times experimentation with such formal qualities as line or perspective lead to a series of works which explore and work out that particular technique. The drawing of the *Angel/Woman* (No. 98) done in 1969, for example, can be compared to such 1969 prints as *Ecclesiast* (1969/52), *Arctic Angel* (1969/53), and *Winter Angel* (1969/54). In these representations of religious subjects, Pudlo is particularly interested in line, and the visual effects to be achieved with linear configurations. In earlier works such as *Woman with Bird Image* (No. 94) or *Spirit with Symbols* (No. 95), he is more concerned with spatial interactions and contrasting dark and light forms. The woman in *Woman with Bird Image*, like the woman of *Angel/Woman*, is the basis for formal experimentation. Another work, the 1974 print *Long Journey* (No. 100), is one in a succession of graphics dealing with perspectival depth and landscape.

Pudlo's works over the years demonstrate his keen visual sense, his versatility and innovativeness in subject matter and technique – tempered by his sense of humour – his knowledge of traditional life on the land, and his acknowledgement of the changing times. While the hunter faces dangerous-looking spirit creatures and evil forces in *Perils of the Hunter* (No. 97), in *The Big Catch* (No. 99) the lucky fisherman has caught a fish many times his size that will no doubt completely swamp him as he lugs it home slung over his shoulder like the man in the 1972 print *Fisherman* (1972/37). Humans carrying loads is a motif used, incidentally, by Pudlo in other works that show, for example, a man carrying a bear (1961/17), another carrying a musk-ox (unpublished drawing), and one man carrying his reluctant bride (1961/16).

Pudlo's thinking/drawing process is a truly creative approach, done both consciously and unconsciously. In the 1978 Cape Dorset print catalogue (p. 67) Pudlo talks about his drawing:

> At times when I draw, I am happy, but sometimes it is very hard. I have been drawing a long time now. I only draw what I think, but sometimes I think the pencil has a brain too.

94.
Pudlo (1916-) m.
Printed by Elijah Pootoogook (1943-) m.
Woman with Bird Image 1961
Stencil 19/50
60.6 x 47.3 cm
78/250

95.
Pudlo (1916-) m.
Printed by Lukta (1928-) m.
Spirit with Symbols 1961
Stonecut 17/50
61.0 x 46.0 cm
78/253

96.
Pudlo (1916-) m.
Printed by Iyola (1933-) m.
Eagle Carrying Man 1963
Stonecut 28/50
62.5 x 48.0 cm
78/290

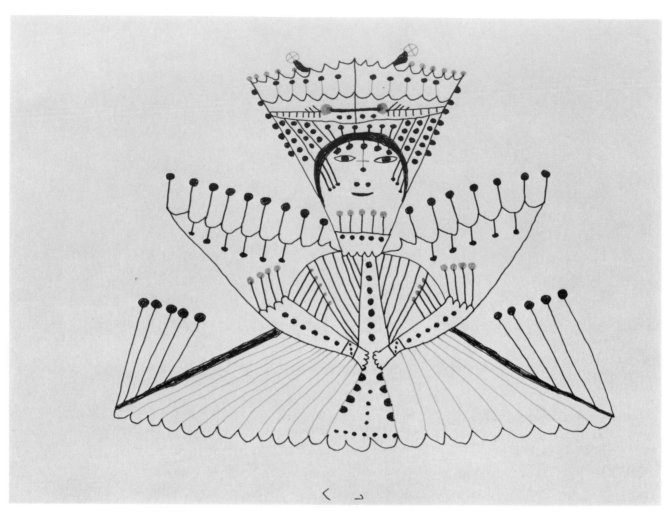

98.
Pudlo (1916-) m.
Angel/Woman 1969
Felt-tip pen
45.7 x 61.1 cm
Signed lower centre with syllabics; dated
   on verso by Cooperative
78/666

97.
Pudlo (1916-) m.
Printed by Lukta (1928-) m.
Perils of the Hunter 1969
Stonecut 18/50
62.5 x 86.8 cm
78/147

99.
Pudlo (1916-) m.
The Big Catch c. 1969
Felt-tip pen
50.8 x 66.2 cm
Signed lower centre with syllabics
78/558

100.
Pudlo (1916-) m.
Printed by Ottochie (1904-1982) m.
Long Journey 1974
Stonecut 47/50
62.6 x 86.4 cm
78/345

Like many contemporary Inuit sculptures, this work (No. 101) was not given a title by the artist. Rather, carvings are subsequently assigned a title – often descriptive in nature – by the dealer, collector, cataloguer, or curator. The title *Dancing Figure Holding His Hair* given to this particular sculpture does describe to a certain extent what is taking place, but there are still puzzling aspects to the representation. Certainly the artist conveys a sense of movement characteristic of a dancing figure, yet it is not clear why the figure is holding his hair, or if in fact the figure is male. Aside from the masculine bulk and the musculature on chest and thighs, the figure is asexual. Perhaps it is a man wearing pants, yet there is no indication of any kind of clothing.

Here, as in his other work, Qavaroak is obviously more interested in form and shape than in narration or realism. Storytelling, proportion, anatomy, clothing, and other details are subordinated to the artist's overall sculptural concerns such as positive/negative space, movement, line, and composition. Qavaroak's depictions of animals, humans, and spirits – usually singly or at most with two to three figures – are often rounded and flowing with an emphasis on curves and lines, particularly the outline of the subjects. Especially in those works comprised of two to three figures, the sculptures can be quite complex, with intertwining and interweaving individual elements. But even the single figures are characterized by curving, rounded, and sensuous lines. In sculptures such as No. 101 and his *Spirit* in the Masterworks exhibition (Canadian Eskimo Arts Council, *Sculpture/Inuit*, No. 335), there is a continuous flow to the line traced around the outside of the figure, around extremities, along backs, and under bodies. Qavaroak tends to work on a heroic grand scale – either the sculptures are physically large or, if not, they are often imbued with a sense of massiveness, weight, and importance – yet the flowing lines and open spaces enliven and enhance the form.

In our sculpture, the heavy dancer is supported by his widely spaced sturdy legs, his feet firmly planted on the base. Nevertheless the sculpture is vigorously alive with suggested and potential movement. The knees bend and push out to the sides tensed with a forthcoming upward bounce, while having one leg bent more than the other throws the weight off the stable vertical axis to an active leaning angle. The bend of the legs is echoed and balanced by the arms curved up to the head. Having the figure hold his hair gets the arms up away from the body and into the action, adding to the interest of the outline and creating additional open spaces.

Qavaroak, or Kabubawakota as he has also been called, has been confused with another artist in Cape Dorset, Kabubuwa Katsiya, who makes graphics (drawing as well as printing) and some carvings. Our artist, Qavaroak the sculptor, is not responsible for any Cape Dorset prints either as draughtsman or printer.

101.
Qavaroak Tunnillie (1928-) m.
Dancing Figure Holding His Hair 1974
Green with black stone
42.5 X 37.3 X 19.5 cm
Signed with syllabics and dated
78/430

Saggiak's rather tentative and inexpert engraving style in no way detracts from the lively, animated hunting scene taking place in this untitled work (No. 102). Bears stride to and fro, dogs bare their teeth, jump and bark while the hunters run, crawl, and shoot at their prey. The lively sense of activity here is accomplished through the poses of the figures as they walk, stride, jump, and crawl, as well as through their placement in the scene – some figures move one way, their neighbours another; some face each other, others move out toward the edge of the paper.

This work is one of only three graphics by Saggiak printed by the Cape Dorset Co-op. Two are engravings from the 1962 collections – the time of experimentation and work in copper-plate engraving which saw prints made by some artists who did little or no graphic work in later years. The third print is a 1966 stonecut *A Hunter's Weapons* printed by Lukta from a Saggiak drawing. According to Patricia Ryan, who is cataloguing the Cape Dorset collection, Saggiak did drawings only in the early years of the graphics program, and then only a small number.

If Saggiak's graphics are few in number and little known, enough of his sculptures are documented to illustrate his consistent concern with certain subjects combined with an overall versatility. Four of Saggiak's sculptures were included in the Masterworks exhibition (Canadian Eskimo Arts Council, *Sculpture/Inuit*, Nos. 230, 311, 348, 357); all depict different subjects, use several different media, and show a keen visual sense. One favourite subject which he thoroughly explored was that of the sea goddess/sea creature (Watt, *Canadian Guild of Crafts Quebec*, Nos. 150, 151; Nelda Swinton, *The Inuit Sea Goddess*, No. 29). Another interesting concern of his was mask-like sculptures of faces (George Swinton, *Sculpture of the Eskimo*, No. 504).

As an older man used to hunting and living in the traditional way, it is not surprising that Saggiak should depict hunters (National Gallery of Canada, *Cape Dorset*, No. 13), even those hunting with the long-outdated bow and arrow as in this print. Originally from the Wakeham Bay area, Saggiak returned there before his death in 1980. His son Kumukulu Saggiak is a well-known Cape Dorset sculptor.

102.
Saggiak (1897-1980) m.
Untitled 1962
Engraving 12/50
33.2 x 48.5 cm
78/261

SHIUQYUK OQUTAQ

Even in Cape Dorset where the sculptors are known for their ability to push the stone medium to its limits, Shiuqyuk's carvings are remarkable for their delicate, fragile lines. Here, the graceful flow of the loon's arched neck and long, lean body (No. 103) is punctuated by the brittlely thin tail feathers, feet, and beak. On the one hand Shiuqyuk works his stone to create realistic details such as the characteristic outlined loon eyes, light-weight feathers, and sharply pointed beaks; on the other hand, he exaggerates and distorts the shape and size of the loon's body. The combination of these two factors – the realistic and the exaggerated – in conjunction with the translucent qualities of the highly polished, attractive green/black stone results in a true-to-life bird, but one more elegant and beautiful than the original.

In recent years Shiuqyuk concentrated on the loon subject in his carvings without becoming repetitive and without entirely neglecting other animal subjects. Although all of the same subject, Shiuqyuk's loons exhibit slight changes and delicate variations on this main theme. Shiuqyuk's carving of loons, fish, dogs, whales, walruses, bears, and the odd human figure was curtailed, however, by his full-time job as the Co-op carpenter, a position he held from 1961 until his death in 1982.

Born near Cape Dorset, Shiuqyuk lived in Sugluk and camps near Cape Dorset and Lake Harbour until the early 1950s when he settled in Lake Harbour. There he worked at boat building for about three years before moving permanently to Cape Dorset with his children and ailing wife in order to be near relatives. Among Shiuqyuk's relatives in Cape Dorset are sculptors Oshuitok, an older brother, and Kumukulu Saggiak, his step-brother.

An early Shiuqyuk carving of an ivory fish dated 1957 in the collection of the Canadian Guild of Crafts (Watt, *Canadian Guild of Crafts Quebec*, No. 92) already shows Shiuqyuk's delicate technique in carving and detailing. The ivory fish, pegged to a stone base and decorated with ink highlights on the fins, gills, eyes, and mouth, is typical of carvings from Lake Harbour at this time. In another sculpture of *Two Sleeping Families* (fig. 17) also in the Guild Collection, Shiuqyuk adds his fine ivory detailing to a poignant stone carving of figures asleep in an igloo. This carving and two others by Shiuqyuk were included in the Masterworks exhibition. One of them, the *Bird with Wings Spread* from about 1960 (Canadian Eskimo Arts Council, *Sculpture/Inuit*, No. 179), also shows Shiuqyuk's carving expertise and penchant for the delicate lines of an elegantly posed bird.

Fig. 17.
Shiuqyuk Oqutaq (1920-1982) m.
Cape Dorset
Two Sleeping Families 1953
Grey stone and ivory
4.0 x 16.5 x 16.5 cm
Canadian Guild of Crafts Quebec

103.
Shiuqyuk Oqutaq (1920-1982) m.
Loon c. 1975
Green/black stone
6.3 x 33.2 x 7.8 cm
Signed with syllabics
78/739

In this engraving (No. 104) and another titled *Man Watching Sea Animals* (1963/55) from the same year, Tuckyashuk fills in his figures with many closely spaced parallel lines. The hunter, his kayak, and prey are all formed from lines that outline the figure, add details, and fill in areas. There is some variation in the length and grouping of the lines where one group stops and another starts, but unlike many other Cape Dorset engravings, there is not the typical variety of burin strokes such as short hatch marks, dots, jagged lines, or U- and V-shapes. Comparison to engravings by Jamasie (Nos. 34-37, 40) or Pauta (Nos. 80-81) illustrates how Tuckyashuk's engraving technique varies from that of others. Using groupings of lines Tuckyashuk does convey a sense of roundness and three-dimensionality in his figures, and if they do not have the texture and shading evident in Jamasie's or Kananginak's animals, they do have an appealing rhythmic unity achieved through their placement and the repetition of line.

Tuckyashuk was not a prolific draughtsman or carver. Three Tuckyashuk prints have been published by the Co-op in Cape Dorset – one stonecut, *The Gathering* showing three figures, in the 1961 collection, and the two 1963 engravings. In all of these works the subjects (people and animals) and action remain fairly simple. The kayak hunter (No. 104) does have some sense of movement and nice touches of detail such as the harpoon at the ready on the kayak's forward harpoon rest. One of Tuckyashuk's carvings from 1953, a female head with tattooed face, is reproduced in George Swinton's book *Eskimo Sculpture* (p. 151). Known to be handy with copper, Tuckyashuk was often commissioned to make harpoon heads and *ulus*, an example of the latter is illustrated in the *Canadian Guild of Crafts Quebec* edited by Virginia Watt (No. 230A).

104.
Tuckyashuk (1898-1972) m.
Kayak Hunter 1963
Engraving 22/50
31.1 X 45.0 cm
78/305

SOLOMONIE TIGULLARAQ

With shoulders and arms pulled back, chest and chin thrust forward, the sea goddess Taleelayo courses through the water. Associated with the sea as her own home and the home of the animals derived from her finger joints, Taleelayo is portrayed here (No. 105) in an aquatic pose like that used in depictions of swimming animals, showing only that part of the animal that rises above the water. Heads and occasionally upper torsos of swimming polar bears, walruses, and caribou cut off at the water line in this manner can be seen in carvings from as far back as the beginning of the Dorset culture (c. 800 BC – c. 1000 AD) and in two- and three-dimensional work by historic and contemporary period artists (fig. 18).

Such a format is not commonly used for representing the sea goddess, but in this small sculpture Tigullaraq has shown how effective it can be. In keeping with this abbreviated pose for the sea-going Taleelayo and in keeping with Tigullaraq's own carving style, details are kept to a minimum; only facial features and the characteristic braid of hair are indicated. With the exception of the eyes, this face has much broader features than are common in other Tigullaraq carvings of people.

Tigullaraq's minimal use of detailing to maximum effect can also be seen in his *Caribou* in the Masterworks exhibition (Canadian Eskimo Arts Council, *Sculpture/Inuit*, No. 141). In this work Tigullaraq's style is much more angular than that of the rounded, tactile sea goddess, but he has used some of the same carving techniques. Starting with a basic caribou shape, he has, by adding only slight facial details and abbreviated horns, and by some distortion of the animal's proportions, managed to convey a *sense* of caribou rather than showing a true-to-life representation.

Tigullaraq's choice of subject matter in the sculpture of the sea goddess is somewhat unusual within not only his own *oeuvre* but that of his community. Tigullaraq's regular subjects are human and animal, not legendary or spiritual ones. Terry Ryan in describing the drawings he collected in 1964 on north Baffin Island, at Clyde River, Pond Inlet, and Arctic Bay, remarked that in contrast to "Cape Dorset [where] many of the drawings depict an interest in the spirit-world . . . this is not the case on north Baffin" (Ryan, "Drawings from the People," pp. 25-27). A continuing emphasis on real animals and people rather than supernatural subjects can be seen in the graphics published in Clyde River's first print collection released in 1981.

Tigullaraq, brother of the Cape Dorset artist Lachaulassie, is recognized in Clyde for his unusual sculptural treatment of usual subjects, showing traditional ideas or themes with a twist. Several examples of this, described in an Indian and Northern Affairs biography of the artist, include Tigullaraq's version of the ever-popular hunting scene in which the tables have been turned and a huge, smiling bear tightly hugs an inconsequentially small man; in another carving, a foot-tapping bear enthusiastically plays an accordian. At one point Tigullaraq's distinctive approach set him apart from his fellow Clyde artists, but if recent sculptures are any indication, others in the community are now following his lead; for example, Alooloo Inutiq's carving of walruses dancing on top of a *kamik*. In a 1969 essay in the files of the Department of Indian and Northern Affairs, a fellow Inuk identifies Tigullaraq as the best carver in Clyde: "His carvings are hard to describe. They are just magnificent."

Fig. 18.
Artist Unknown
Pelly Bay
Hunter and Bear c. 1970
Whalebone, hide, and baleen
8.5 x 14.8 x 10.0 cm
Art Gallery of Ontario
Gift of the Klamer Family, 1978

105.
Solomonie Tigullaraq (1924-) m.
Sea Goddess c. 1973
Dark green stone
8.0 x 10.0 x 6.3 cm
Signed with Roman
78/629

LUKE ANAUTALIK

The motif of human heads clustered together in a group is especially prevalent in carvings from the west coast of Hudson Bay. Although the subject does occasionally appear elsewhere, it is never as popular in other communities as it is in Eskimo Point, Rankin Inlet, and Baker Lake. Interpretations of these multiple human heads – a sculptural subject that dates as far back as the prehistoric Dorset culture – range from family or community portrait, to depiction of spirit beings, to simply a good subject for a saleable carving.

Of the possible interpretations it seems likely that the Anautalik heads and partial figures are spirits congregating on a piece of antler that is itself animated with emerging spirit faces. Spirits, in all shapes and forms, traditionally have been believed to appear singly or in groups everywhere in the Arctic. Some were well enough known to be given tribal names; some were reputed to have special abilities or characteristics; some lived in particular places; some were evil; others acted as shamanic helpers. Everything, animate or inanimate, also had its spirit, often represented in art works by a diminutive face. Regardless of what particular type of spirit they are, these wonderful little rudimentary figures and heads on this carving do look more supernatural than human.

This sculpture (No. 106) is quite similar to another by Anautalik dated 1970 and illustrated in George Swinton's book *Sculpture of the Eskimo* (No. 592). In that sculpture similar spirit creatures appear above and below the antler base which, as in this sculpture, acts as a curving, multi-pronged ground area by utilizing the natural shape of the antler. Unlike the Swinton one, however, in this work the artist has articulated some of the antler tips with faces; he has also, in several cases, further defined the spirit bodies with little attached arms tied on with sinew. The perky, alert character of the figures and faces, and the fact that an antler tip may unexpectedly be transformed into a tiny figure with moveable arms give the sculpture a significant level of animation illustrating the common Eskimo belief that everything has its spirit – everything lives!

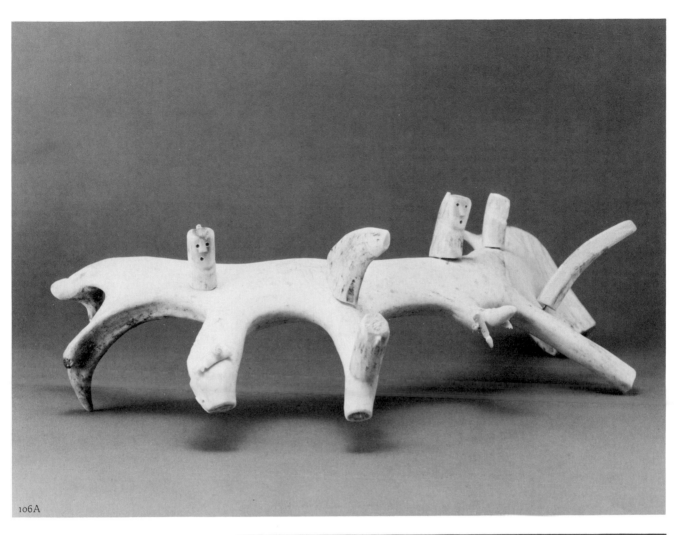

106A

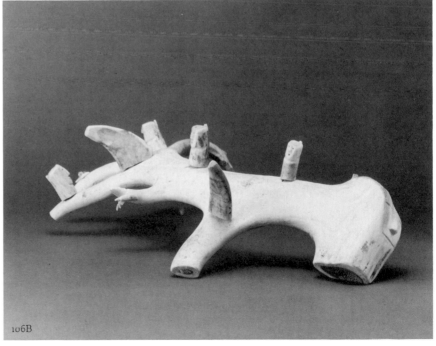

106B

106.
Luke Anautalik (1932-) m.
Spirits c. 1972
Antler and sinew
10.9 x 34.8 x 21.0 cm
Unsigned
78/231

LOUIS ARVIYUT

Working with his hard grey stone Louis Arviyut has, with only some surface definition and a bit of added material, created an expressive and effective portrayal of a figure carrying a bulky, cumbersome, and heavy load on his back (No. 107). The grooves filed into the bundle and the man's head provide a channel for the sinew lashing while also indicating the cutting tension of the supported weight. And the little scrap of hide on the figure's forehead shows in realistic detail how padding is used to soften the abrasive pull of the cordage. Even the man's eyebrows seem to be pulled into a straight line with the concentration and concerted effort required to trudge along with his burden which he steadies in place with one arm.

At the time this piece was done, Eskimo Point artists were using a grey stone for their carving. Unlike the softer stone from, say, the opposite side of Hudson Bay which is more easily modelled, incised, and polished, this grey stone is so hard that it is difficult to work. The hardness of their stone has affected the type of carving done by people in Eskimo Point, resulting in less detail and surface definition, as well as a rougher finish.

Thus, Louis Arviyut has devoted his attention to the distinctive aspects of his figure – the face (achieved with slight elevation to the nose, drilled nostril holes, raised hairline and filed out features), the bundle, and the rudimentary arms. The lower torso simply rounds out and finishes the body as a base area. The added materials of sinew and hide embellish and make an important addition to the main thrust of the sculpture; they are realistic details that in sculptures from other communities might have been incorporated into a softer stone. The still visible file marks and the emphasis on essentials give the sculpture a freshness and immediacy, which successfully conveys to us the essence of this everyday activity.

107.
Louis Arviyut (1941-) m.
Man Carrying Burden on Back c. 1970
Grey stone, hide, and sinew
11.0 X 11.2 X 4.7 cm
Signed with syllabics
78/723

107A

107B

LUKE HALLAUK

In keeping with the gaunt leanness of this mother and child sculpture (No. 108), the head of the child in the mother's parka faces in the wrong direction, as though positioning it facing forward (as it normally should be) would unnecessarily complicate and disrupt the terribly thin lines. The baby's wedge-shaped face looking in one direction opposes the sharp angle of the mother's facial features that create a ridge down the centre of her face; this ridge is continued by the shoulders and long, thin arms pinched forward down the length of her body. The arms terminate as they merge into the lower edge of her parka that in turn flows around the figure who is seated with her legs drawn up under her in traditional fashion.

Like the other Eskimo Point sculptures included here there is little definition to the stone surface. File marks are readily apparent, especially on the woman's head – possibly to simulate her hair. Certainly her hairline is clearly indicated around the edge of her face while the baby's face is outlined with a continuous line. Both their facial features are deeply and definitely articulated. A comparison of this simple but appealing version of the mother and child theme with the others from Eskimo Point demonstrates that the face and hair and to some extent the mother's arms and parka are the important details; these are the key features of the depiction even though they are more roughly defined than they would be in sculptures of similar subjects from other areas.

108.
Attributed to
Luke Hallauk (1931-) m.
Mother and Child c. 1972
Dark grey stone
10.0 X 2.5 X 7.2 cm
Unsigned
78/238

ELIZABETH NOOTARALOO

The baby with its bottle gives an unexpected detail to this otherwise typical Eskimo Point sculpture (No. 109). The mother is shown with legs folded under her body, a pose customary in real life and common in Inuit sculpture. The width of her chest and the widely spaced arms and legs, combined with the depth of her body, make the woman a substantial and stable figure; the massiveness is lightly accented by the small open space between the baby's bottle and the woman's body below. Again the obviously important details are the definition of the face, the hairline, and the parka, even though the parka edge is roughly articulated and the baby's hair somewhat plate-like. Yet the nostrils are indicated with carefully done little round holes, and the spreading fingers of the hand are separated by incised lines, a motif often found in Nootaraloo's sculptures.

A whalebone bird by Nootaraloo – quite different from the present sculpture – was included in the Masterworks exhibition (Canadian Eskimo Arts Council, *Sculpture/Inuit*, No. 169). Much more common in her work is the typical mother and child, sometimes with some atypical characteristics such as this baby with its bottle, or as another carving that has a rounded base enabling the sculptural mother to rock her child.

109.
Elizabeth Nootaraloo (1914-) f.
Mother and Child 1967
Grey stone
23.8 x 14.8 x 17.4 cm
Signed with disc number
78/226

Susan Ootnooyuk, working with the typical hard, dull grey stone of Eskimo Point, has accented it in an unusual, feminine way (No. 110). Necklaces and earrings were not traditional forms of adornment for Eskimo women, although caribou teeth were a type of jewellery or decoration threaded together and sewn onto belts or parkas. Beads, and other foreign objects such as coins, once they became available in the Arctic through trade and outside contact, were used as decoration on women's parkas. They were threaded for fringe, sewn into front panels and trimming for cuffs, shoulders, and edges.

Beadwork of this type can be seen in several photographs of Eskimo women from the early 1900s as in *The Inuit Amautik* exhibition catalogue (Driscoll, *The Inuit Amautik* pp. 6, 10). Niviatsianaq is dressed in a particularly elaborate style (fig. 19; originally identified in the records as Shoofly Comer, an identification subsequently corrected by Ms. Driscoll). Her attire illustrates how the Eskimo women adapted new forms of personal adornment such as beads, earrings, and rings and integrated them with traditional ones such as caribou teeth ornamentation, facial tattooing, hair bindings, and parka decoration.

Necklaces and earrings became more common attire over the years, but they have never been prevalent in sculptural or graphic representations, indicative, perhaps, of their insignificance or their inappropriateness as far as the artists are concerned. Many artists still tend to portray more traditional scenes, excluding new items such as the ubiquitous western style clothes, snowmobiles, and airplanes. Ootnooyuk's use of jewellery here is not unique for her; her carving in the Masterworks exhibition (Canadian Eskimo Arts Council, *Sculpture/Inuit*, No. 387) shows a double figure of two women, each with a bead necklace and earrings. In the sculpture illustrated here the necklace, especially, is a focal point, encircling the round, high cheek-boned face that is surmounted by the unusually elevated child behind. Attention is focussed on this disproportionately large face, the jewellery, and the child, rather than on the somewhat slab-like body beneath with its rudimentary extremities and long parka flap.

Fig. 19.
Photograph of Niviatsianaq (1903-04)
(A.P. Low Expedition, 1903-04)
Public Archives Canada/PA 53548

110. Opposite
Susan Ootnooyuk (1918- c. 1975) f.
Mother Wearing Necklace and Earrings
c. 1970
Grey stone, caribou teeth, beads, and sinew
22.0 x 7.6 x 6.3 cm
Signed with syllabics
78/724
See colour plate on page 25.

Lucy Tasseor has identified her characteristic groupings of human faces as men, women, and children, or just heads. In this sculpture (No. 111) the slight indication of arms related to the figure at the back suggests that this is a mother and her children. In Tasseor's sculptures the emphasis on heads predominates; arms are sometimes defined but other anatomical features are rarely shown.

Of the five Tasseor sculptures included in the Masterworks exhibition, only one, *Man* (Canadian Eskimo Arts Council, *Sculpture/Inuit*, No. 393), depicts a sole human subject or gives any real indication of a torso and rudimentary legs; the others show only human heads or heads in a grouping with some indication of arms as in this sculpture. In her synecdochical style, however, Tasseor still conveys a sense of family or togetherness through the curving forms and the closeness, small size, and repetition of the typical head motif. The faces of these heads are consistently similar with the same ridged nose and horizontal lines of varying lengths for the eyes and mouth, making a Tasseor sculpture readily identifiable.

111.
Lucy Tasseor (1934-) f.
Mother and Children c. 1972
Dark grey stone
14.8 x 14.2 x 6.3 cm
Signed with syllabics
78/237

EVE UKATNA

Although it is not at all unusual to show only the child's head rising up out of the *amaut* at the back of the mother's parka, it is unusual to find a lone head in front of the woman as in this sculpture (No. 112). The head itself is virtually identical in features to that of the mother and the two flat faces are inclined at a similar angle at the same height above the surrounding area. This similarity unites the two people just as the mother's encircling arms bring them closer together in a protective, motherly gesture.

Perhaps the mother is simply holding the child or more practically, perhaps he is being held out in front of her to relieve himself. The bulge of the woman's parka and the protruding head, however, suggest that the child is beneath the parka. And certainly mothers would move their child to the inside front of the parka more often than the standard sculptural format would suggest. Children were regularly transferred up front for nursing or to facilitate the mother's actions or movements (as in the Belcher Island carving titled *Crawling Woman with Child*, illustrated in Driscoll, *The Inuit Amautik*, p. 51). Shifting the child from back to front could be accomplished by lifting him out of the *amaut* and putting him back inside the parka at the front, or simply by shifting him from back to front inside the loosely fitted garment – a technique especially suitable for very cold conditions. Facing outward as he is, this child is certainly not nursing, but perhaps on a less literal level of interpretation, the sculpture represents a woman dreaming of motherhood, actually pregnant, or giving birth. Regardless of what specific act may be represented here – and it is unnecessary to try to pin down one interpretation – the format of the sculpture totally conveys the interaction and close protective union between a mother and her child.

112.
Eve Ukatna (1941-) f.
Mother and Child c. 1970
Dark grey stone
10.0 x 8.4 x 9.4 cm
Signed with syllabics
78/703

NUVEEYA IPELLIE

In a short autobiographical statement in the files of the Department of Indian and Northern Affairs, Nuveeya writes, "I don't make carvings all the time. I work at the Frobisher Bay Jewellery Workshop. It's good working there." And in 1976, the same year that the present sculpture was made, his entry won an award of merit in the northern jewellery competition *The Things That Make Us Beautiful.* Nuveeya's interest in jewellery and his ability to work with precision and delicacy on such a small scale can be seen in his treatment of the sea goddess's eyes in this sculpture (No. 113). Jewellers in places like Frobisher Bay and Cape Dorset work with imported semi-precious stones as well as such indigenous materials as the ivory and baleen used here. Multiple inset eyes of this nature are a recurring note in Nuveeya's carvings of the late 1970s and early 1980s. A particularly striking example of Nuveeya's jewel and dental work is the 1977 *Bear Head* in the collection of the Canada Council Art Bank (fig. 20).

Northern jewellers also make use of attractive stones like the deep green one of this sculpture (No. 113), and Nuveeya's treatment of the stone in his carving has a certain jewel-like character in the lustrous smooth polish of the body and the filigree-like detailing on the tail and, to a lesser degree, the hands. Adding to the elegance of this piece is the graceful curve of the figure's upturned body, climaxing in an arched sweep of the tail, slightly turned and spiralling the movement up and off the inner tip of the tail.

There are several other published examples of Nuveeya's treatment of the sea goddess subject such as in the catalogue *The Inuit Sea Goddess* (Nelda Swinton, No. 26) and on an invitation for a Nuveeya and Seepee (his son) Ipellie exhibition at the Waddington Gallery in Toronto in 1979. These two sculptures, the first dated 1974, the other presumably close in date to the exhibition (1979), can be compared to our 1976 carving, demonstrating Nuveeya's concern with the sea goddess subject over a number of years. In format the three works are very similar – the sea creature lies on her side, her arms to the front with flippers spread on her chest, and her body and tail curved up in a U (although in the 1974 sculpture the tail is extended up to the face, closing the gap between head and tail). Of the three, the Klamer piece displays more elegance in form, polish and detail such as the inset eyes. The faces of all figures are by no means beautiful. Her broad nose and wide lips can be compared with those of the sea goddess by Tigullaraq of Clyde River (No. 105). Perhaps these sculptures echo those versions of the Taleelayo legend in which the sea goddess is described as ugly.

On the other hand, these less than beautiful faces may reflect Nuveeya's approach to his subjects. Comparing these sea goddesses, the bear head, and a walrus in the Art Bank Collection and a musk-ox in the collection of the Department of Indian and Northern Affairs, it is apparent that Nuveeya is less concerned with the actual physical beauty of the subject than with the beauty of its form. These sculptures are characterized by elegance, high polish, and fine details such as the bear teeth, musk-ox horn, and walrus tusks. The animals are not accurately proportioned or particularly naturalistic; the bear's nose is the wrong shape and too long, the walrus is too long and thin, and the musk-ox is more like a grand dame in her ankle-length ball gown. The strength of Nuveeya's sculptures – and strength they do have – comes not so much

Fig. 20.
Nuveeya Ipellie (1920-) m.
Frobisher Bay
Bear Head 1977
Light green stone, dark green stone, ivory, and baleen
15.5 x 10.5 x 10.0 cm
Canada Council Art Bank, Ottawa

from the accuracy of his representations as from his expressive treatment of the actual form and media.

Nuveeya was born in Lake Harbour and lived in Pangnirtung and Cape Dorset before settling in Frobisher Bay in 1945. In 1959 he spent about a year in hospital in Hamilton, Ontario. According to Nuveeya he was taught carving by his late father Ennutsiak whose work is well known, especially the carvings that illustrate traditional birth scenes. Nuveeya's first carving was a female figure done in whalebone; as he says in his biographical statement, "I like to carve figures best."

113.
Nuveeya Ipellie (1920-) m.
Sea Goddess 1976
Dark green stone, ivory, and baleen
22.5 x 26.0 x 10.9 cm
Signed with Roman and dated
78/644
See colour plate on page 22.

JOSIE NAPARTUK

The merging of animal and human forms is not uncommon in sculpture from Great Whale River. Generally working on a small scale, as Josie Napartuk has here, artists such as Mina Tooktoo and Josie's son, Henry Napartuk, show composite scenes where the different animal and human elements are united in one integrated, often complex form; a woman's head merges with a claw and feet or hands are joined to human heads (Canadian Eskimo Arts Council, *Sculpture/Inuit*, No. 324 and 326). In one sculpture (The Winnipeg Art Gallery, *The Zazelenchuk Collection of Eskimo Art*, No. 88), Henry Napartuk has combined bird and human forms in a composition somewhat similar to the carving illustrated here (No. 114).

In Josie Napartuk's sculpture a man's face, outlined by the fur trim on his parka hood, is carved into one side of a three-dimensional, fully-fashioned bird. Although the bird is a complete unit on its own, the fact that the human face appears only on one side focusses attention on this view. The bird's raised wings with streamlined, incised lines convey the sense of potential movement, in some contrast to the straightforward frontal face below.

The conjunction of bird and human face in the sculpture may well be associated with shamanism, even though the transformations shown in Great Whale River sculpture usually seem to be related more to artistic concerns than spiritual ones. The union of bird and human being is a popular motif in shamanistic representation, illustrating the shaman's ability to fly and his close association with the animal world through his own transformation into animal form and communication with the animals, as well as their role as his helping spirits. Another possible interpretation is suggested by the common practice in art works of using a small human face to represent the individual spirit or *inua* that traditionally inhabited each object, being, and place.

114.
Josie Napartuk (1901-1980) m.
Great Whale River
Bird and Human Face c. 1969
Dark green stone
11.5 X 15.5 X 3.2 cm
Signed with syllabics
78/692

INUKJUAK
(Port Harrison)

JOE ADLIKIT ACULIAK

Like his carving of a *Fish* included in the Masterworks exhibition (Canadian Eskimo Arts Council, *Sculpture/Inuit*, No. 154), and like much of the work done in Inukjuak, Joe's *Walrus* (No. 115) is not a heroic or momentous subject, but it is a true-to-life representation. As Paulosie Kasadluak wrote in a 1976 essay entitled "Nothing Marvellous" for an exhibition of Inukjuak sculpture (The Winnipeg Art Gallery, *Port Harrison/Inoucdjouac*, p. 21):

> We carve the animals because they are important to us as food. We carve Inuit figures because in that way we can show ourselves to the world as we were in the past and as we now are. That is why we carve men hunting and building igloos and women making something that they will use, maybe sewing kamiks or clothing or using an ulu. No matter what activity the carved figure is engaged in, something about it will be true. That is because we carve to show what we have done as people. There is nothing marvellous about it. It is there for everyone to see. It is just the truth.

According to Barry Roberts (*The Inuit Artists of Inoucdjouac, P.Q.*, p. 36), Joe is a prolific carver, most of whose works represent people. Illustrations of Joe's sculpture in George Swinton's book *Sculpture of the Eskimo* (No. 139) and in the Winnipeg Art Gallery exhibition catalogue *Port Harrison/Inoucdjouac* (Nos. 11, 12) demonstrate that he is also an accomplished carver of animal subjects as was his late father Aculiak who seemed to specialize in numerous and sometimes odd or humorous, but always accurate, carvings of animals. Certainly the *Walrus* included here illustrates Joe's ability to portray a life-like walrus, with characteristic features such as the whiskers and tusks as well as the naturalistic pose with head cocked to one side. Even on this small scale, the overall shape, the supportive position of the flippers, and the folds of fat at the neck suggest the weight and bulk of a life-size walrus.

The suggested size of this realistic walrus, however, is tempered by the actual sculptural size and form which make him eminently touchable and appealing. The warm appeal of these Inukjuak pieces is much like one's impression of the actual settlement, where even the first visit is more like a homecoming.

115.
Joe Adlikit Aculiak (1936-) m.
Walrus 1960s
Black stone and ivory
4.0 x 8.7 x 5.2 cm
Signed with syllabics and disc number
78/674

Scenes such as this (No. 116) and the similar one by Nayoumealook (No. 118) are classic examples of the domestic and narrative nature of Inukjuak sculpture showing, as Paulosie Kasadluak has said, "what we have done as people" (The Winnipeg Art Gallery, *Port Harrison/Inoucdjouac*, p. 21). Here, a mother with a child in her *amautiq* prepares food in front of her *kudlik*.

The low flickering flame of the burning wick along the edge of the lamp is represented by the toothed length of bone attached to the stone. Addition of complementary materials enabled the Port Harrison sculptors to create a greater sense of verisimilitude, to embellish their stone surface, and to fill in or add on to their stone area. In this sculpture, the already rich and lustrous dark green stone is further enhanced by the addition of the woman's inset face and attached ivory hands. The light green stone face, set against the woman's dark hair, is delicate and finely featured even to the extent of the eyebrows thinly pencilled in with blacking. The woman's ivory hands emerge from stone arms that seem to terminate somewhat abruptly. Evident between the first and second fingers of her right hand is what looks like the shaft of an *ulu* which has since broken off.

Elijassiapik's use of insets and ivory additions to his stone sculpture can also be seen in his *Bird* included in the Masterworks exhibition (Canadian Eskimo Arts Council, *Sculpture/Inuit*, No. 175) where the bird has inset ivory and stone eyes and attached ivory claws on each foot. In the Klamer sculpture, the auxiliary materials give the artist a certain degree of freedom in his work since the entire sculpture, with the exception of the unusually small seal in the bowl, is carved from a single piece of stone.

The way the woman is seated – her legs forming a wide U beside and in front of her – and the way the large, flat base from which she is carved flows out around her emphasize her weight and massiveness. The rounded shape of her lower body is echoed by the circle of her open hood forming a wide, flat area from which the neckless heads rise; they emerge from the mass below almost as abruptly as her ivory hands do from their stone arms. These features accentuate her solidity, and in spite of her somewhat misplaced, bumpy breasts the woman remains a personification of earth-mother provider.

Elijassiapik's treatment of the mother figure can be compared to that of his brother Johnny Inukpuk who, as the more productive carver, is the better known. We often see in Inukpuk's sculptures of a mother and child this same concern with archetypal womanhood. Elijassiapik, who died in the early 1970s, was not a prolific carver. The style of this particular sculpture suggests that it was done in the 1950s.

116.
Elijassiapik (1912-1972) m.
Mother and Child with Kudlik 1950s
Dark green stone, ivory, light green stone,
    black stone, bone, and blacking
14.0 X 21.5 X 24.7 cm
Signed with syllabics and disc number
78/433
See colour plate on page 28.

ABRAHAM NASTAPOKA

The bear subjects in this sculpture (No. 117) and their style of presentation belong to a trend in Inukjuak carvings during the 1950s when the artists produced stone candlesticks, salt and pepper shakers, and bookends in the form of various animals. Bears were a popular choice; positioned on end, as in this sculpture, they supported books or candles, or had holes in the top of their heads for dispensing spices. That these bears remain fixed together, despite the suggestion of a dividing line between them to make matching ends, indicates that function was not always the prime concern. A comparable bookend by Aculiak in the collection of the Winnipeg Art Gallery (*Port Harrison/Inoucdjouac*, No. 9) does have a space between the two ends, but in this case the ends cannot be moved since the whole unit is carved out of one piece of stone. As a result the unadjustable space of about half an inch between is suitable perhaps for a couple of files, but hardly for books.

Presumably the Nastapoka bears were never meant to act as a pair of bookends. Technically it would have been much easier to separate them before completing the carving and polishing. And these bears are finished, down to such details as the small incised marks for claws on their feet and incised dots for whiskers on their snouts. Perhaps this unit is one end of a pair, but it is more likely that although inspired by the format of more functional models, they were not intended for use as such.

Nastapoka's handling of stone can also be seen in his sculpture of a human head included in the Masterworks exhibition (Canadian Eskimo Arts Council, *Sculpture/Inuit*, No. 366; George Swinton, *Eskimo Sculpture*, p. 82 for colour). Here, firmly controlling the overpowering rich green and orange stone, he has carved a striking and powerful head.

According to Barry Roberts (*The Inuit Artists of Inoucdjouac, P.Q.*, pp. 58-59), Nastapoka took his last name from the river south of Inukjuak where he operated a canteen before the Second World War. Once a recognized camp leader and hunter, Nastapoka was described even in his seventies as a "real man" by his fellow Inuit. Trouble with his arms forced him to give up carving in 1974.

117.
Abraham Nastapoka (1900-1981) m.
Two Bears 1950s
Dark green stone and whitening
18.4 X 10.1 X 10.1 cm
Unsigned
78/633

117A

117B

NAYOUMEALOOK

Working with a similar subject and format as Elijassiapik in his sculpture (No. 116), Nayoumealook has created quite a different effect in *Woman Cutting Up Fish* (No. 118). Again the entire sculpture is carved from one piece of stone, but the woman's relationship to the base has changed. Here she kneels at the edge of the sculpture base which supports the *kudlik* and the food being cut up. She is an extension of the base, not an element on it, and her individuality is further indicated by the open space between her legs and the base. The greater height of the lamp at the front of the arrangement counteracts to some extent the weight of the female figure, thus focussing more attention on the actual activity taking place and less on the woman herself.

Nayoumealook's interest in domestic activities can also be seen in his sculpture of a *Woman Stretching and Shaping Boot* (Driscoll, *The Inuit Amautik*, p. 55) where a bulky woman with a child in her *amautiq* leans forward to work on a *kamik* upturned on a vertical support. In comparing the mother and child in the boot scene to the woman in the present carving, one is struck by the absence of the ubiquitous child. No little face peers forth from the folds of the mother's parka here, but the typical slightly off centre shape of the pulled up hood – and our expectations – ensure that there must be a small figure snuggled down inside.

But Nayoumealook does not break the flat surface at the front of the hood to show us the baby or even the mother's neck and shoulders. Instead what would be an open area between the head and the inner edge of the hood is left intact and the woman's face becomes a bas-relief on a flat surface. The centrally parted hair, high cheekbones, and delicate features of her face gently rise from the background. In contrast to the broader features of the woman's face in *Woman Stretching and Shaping Boot* where the three-dimensional, fully defined head is shown above a down-turned hood, here the woman's facial features seem to have been refined and softened in keeping with their emergence from a flat background.

118A

118.
Nayoumealook (1891-1966) m.
Woman Cutting Up Fish 1950s
Green-black stone and bone
14.3 X 13.5 X 23.7 cm
Signed with syllabics and disc number
78/623

118B

JOSIE NOWRA

We have no way of knowing now whether these two bird heads (No. 119) were intended as a pair or not. Each is individually signed with the artist's disc number and name – Josie on one, Mr. Josie on the other – so they could have been considered separate, but their complementary size and identical form suggest that they were meant to go together.

The heads are highly polished, the smooth black surface interrupted only by the tasteful contrast of inset light green eyes. The eyes help to orient our view of the heads as well as helping us to identify the subject, since the shape of the heads and beaks, their simplicity and stark elegance, have a certain element of abstraction.

There are no other readily accessible published examples of sculptures by Josie, who died in 1976, but a very similar work of the same subject by Amidlak also of Inukjuak provides an interesting comparison (fig. 21). The shape of beak in the Amidlak is almost identical to that of the Nowra birds, while realistic details such as the eye with pupil, the incised feathers, the nostril hole in the beak, and the shape of the head make the Amidlak bird more realistic than the Nowra pair. Comparison of the heads clearly points up the abstract quality of the ones by Nowra. Nowra's birds were originally undated, but the obvious similarity in format suggests that the works could be contemporaneous. Inuit artists still, in a deceivingly nonchalant way, assess their fellow artists' work on the Hudson's Bay Company or Co-op storage shelves, and are always open to a good idea.

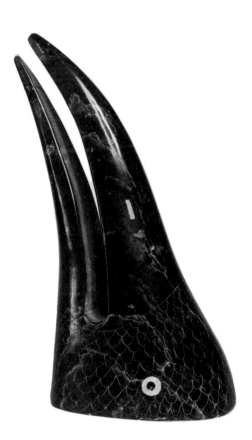

Fig. 21.
Amidlak (1897-1961) m.
Inukjuak
Head of a Bird 1954
Dark green stone and ivory
18.0 x 10.5 x 6.5 cm
Department of Indian Affairs and
    Northern Development, Ottawa

119.
Josie Nowra (1917-1976) m.
Two Bird Heads 1950s
Black stone and light green stone
a. 12.8 x 9.1 x 2.9 cm
b. 10.5 x 8.6 x 2.7 cm
Signed with Roman and disc number
78/431

a.

b.

JOANASSIE OOMAYOUALOOK

The size, stance, and broad facial features of the figure help explain the original mistitling of this piece as a hunter with his catch. Certainly the figure, which does not look very feminine, holds the captured, limp goose more as a successful hunter would than as a woman preparing the meat for a meal. Nevertheless, that this is a woman is proven by her standard female-style parka. Perhaps she has just caught the goose herself. Traditionally women hunted fish and birds on their own or as part of a group effort when the prey was pursued into ambush. During moulting season the geese, unable to fly, were simply run to ground. In any event, this proud and impressive woman with her captured goose could easily be titled *Huntress with Catch*.

The subject matter of this sculpture is in keeping with Oomayoualook's *oeuvre* which has been described by Barry Roberts in *The Inuit Artists of Inoucdjouac, P.Q.* (p. 67) as people at traditional activities and animals posed in action.

120.
Joanassie Oomayoualook (1934-) m.
Woman with Goose 1960s
Black stone
24.3 x 18.8 x 19.7 cm
Signed with syllabics and disc number
78/439

SHORTY KILLIKTEE

Balanced on one foot, a strange spirit creature holds its equally strange little offspring. Carved in characteristic green Lake Harbour stone, the two figures are articulated with similar markings – incised almond-shaped eyes with circular pupils, hollowed out nostrils and mouths, and unusual round or tear-drop-shaped cavities which effectively represent, in reverse, their claws. Both creatures also have inset ivory tongues, while the adult has additional ivory horns and little spikes sprouting from its head. Bizarre in appearance as these creatures may be, they are nevertheless endearing. The cute little junior model is clasped to its parent's body as the Inuk child is held by the mother in so many carvings.

In all respects this sculpture resembles carvings of the same subject that are attributed to another Lake Harbour artist, Nuyaliaq Qimirqpik, or Newquilliak (George Swinton, *Sculpture of the Eskimo*, No. 517; Surrey Art Gallery, *Sculpture of the Inuit*, No. B-50). According to the 1970 Lake Harbour disc list in the files of the Inuit Art Section of Indian and Northern Affairs, the two artists – Shorty and Newquilliak – are brothers, and in 1970 they and their wives are listed as sharing a house. Perhaps, the two brothers, living in the same household about the time that this work was done, influenced one another's style. Other examples of Shorty's work (unpublished) show different subjects and sculptural concerns than this carving while examples of Newquilliak's work (unpublished) show that he too has done carvings of animals and incised scenes totally different in approach from his spirit figures. Certainly this piece is signed with the artist's first name in Roman and his disc number. Recent inquiries in Lake Harbour have established that there is no question that this sculpture was done by Shorty.

Confusion over authorship and mix-ups in attribution have been a problem in Inuit art since the days when one person came in from camp to sell work done by others to a purchaser who might not know the seller or the carver by name. Other times, confusion has resulted from cooperative artistic ventures on the part of husband and wife or members of the same family, or when the work of one family member resembles that of another. There have also been instances when the work of one individual has been signed by another. Precise attribution, so important to many others, is not as pressing a concern for many Inuit.

121.
Shorty Killiktee (1949-) m.
Spirit with Young c. 1969
Green stone and ivory
24.5 X 14.3 X 14.4 cm
Signed with Roman and disc number
78/686
See colour plate on page 32.

The top of her parka pulled down below her arms, perhaps to facilitate nursing, an Inuk woman holds her child in her arms. The child's body, which seems about to slide off the mother's lap to one side, is balanced by the bulky folds of her parka on the other side. While the woman's extended foot and spreading parka build up a wide, solid base for the sculpture, the child's position off to one side sets up a sense of tension within the work that is reinforced by the curving, undulating, and busy lines of the arms, legs, parka folds, and clothing details of the two intersecting bodies.

Further visual variety is provided by the open spaces around the base between the feet, the parka, and the surface the sculpture rests on. And although some carvings by Mosesee have the solid, static qualities of this sculpture, the interest in open areas and the emphasis on tension and curving forms are characteristic of several other published examples of his work. Both his 1970 carving of two men wrestling (Canadian Eskimo Arts Council, *Sculpture*, unpaged) and the 1977 sculpture of *Woman Stretching a Boot* (Agnes Etherington Art Centre, *Inuit Art in the 1970's*, No. 39) show figures moving up and out from a firm base, their arms and legs creating intersecting open spaces. In the *Woman Stretching a Boot*, especially, the artist emphasizes the open work between child, mother, and boot.

In contrast to these sculptures, however, much of the fluidity of movement in our sculpture takes place over the surface area of the two figures rather than between them. The mother's face in particular, too, is done with unusual sensitivity as shown by the contrasting black inset pupils, the rounded, modelled, and realistic Eskimoan face, and the fine lines incised for her eyebrows and hair.

An earlier work by Mosesee, an ivory tusk dated 1963 in the Winnipeg Art Gallery (*The Bessie Bulman Collection*, No. 59), shows similar attention to detail in the northern motifs which are incised with a variety of fine markings into the surface of the walrus tusk. A prolific carver, Mosesee began carving in 1942; he was taught, he says, by his father Kolola.

Born near Lake Harbour where he now resides, Mosesee has also lived in Frobisher Bay. He has been active in local and community affairs in Lake Harbour as President of the Cooperative and the settlement council; in 1978 he was elected to the Board of Directors of Canadian Arctic Producers, Ottawa. This position as well as earlier hospitalization have necessitated a number of trips to the south.

122.
Mosesee Kolola (1930-   ) m.
Mother and Child c. 1977
Green stone and black stone
31.5 x 35.8 x 31.2 cm
Unsigned
78/740

SIMEONA ARNAKRETUAR

Heroic neither in scale nor subject this little dog nevertheless alertly goes about his important – at least to him – canine business. Legs astride and head erect, his outstretched tail continues the straight line of his back and emphasizes his movement forward.

Many Inuit artists excel in such life-like and sensitive depictions of mundane, everyday subjects, making them just as eloquent as more dramatic ones.

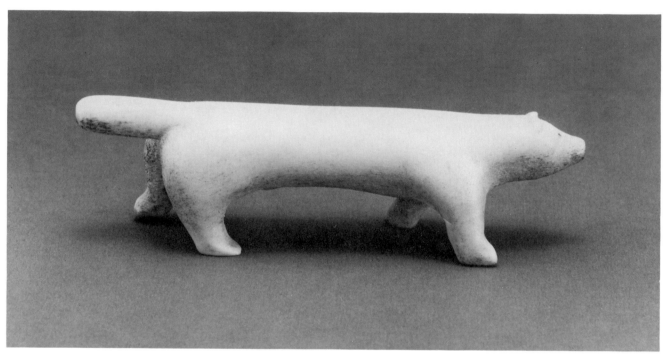

123.
Simeona Arnakretuar (1926-   ) f.
Dog c. 1967
Bone and blacking
3.3 X 11.0 X 3.0 cm
Unsigned
78/702

ZACHARIE ITTIMANGNAQ

The formal, static pose of these figures and their conjunction at the two ends of the antler base give this sculpture a composed, ritualistic air. The man with a child on his shoulders and the bear with a cub at his legs balance and even oppose each other in the scene (No. 124).

Bears were traditionally held in high esteem by Eskimos. They were ferocious opponents in the hunt and they were, of all the arctic animals, the most like human beings in character and form, especially when they stood upright on their hind legs. Bears were considered to be the most powerful helping spirits a shaman could have, and several contemporary art works show the spirit bear flying through the air with a shaman on his back. While in flight the bear stretched his head forward and held his forelegs at his side as the bear cub does in the sculpture illustrated on page 192 (No. 124).

The position of this cub, in fact, is virtually identical to that of contemporary sculptures of flying bears (fig. 22) and their predecessors (fig. 23), the shamanic bears from the prehistoric Canadian Dorset culture (c. 800 BC – c. 1000 AD). Aside from the markings, our cub greatly resembles the older bear (fig. 23), originally found at a Dorset site in the Igloolik area not far from Pelly Bay. From another Dorset culture site in the same area comes a carving comparable to the other two figures in the Ittimangnaq sculpture (No. 124) – a man with a child on his shoulders (fig. 24). The similarity here is tantalizing but the subject matter is so common that this similarity of pose is probably not significant.

While Zacharie Ittimangnaq's sculptural treatment of his subjects gives this carving a formalized ritualism, it seems unlikely that the work as a whole holds any special meaning. It seems more likely that the artist's depiction of poses so similar to those from prehistoric times, some of which would at that time have had religious significance, is an instance of old images resurfacing in the work of contemporary artists who themselves can give no explanation of the image or its source. It is as though the modern artists unconsciously and unwittingly produce visual images – no longer meaningful to them – that are faint echoes of religious beliefs from their distant past.

Fig. 22.
Artist Unknown
Povungnituk
Bear from the sculpture *Shaman Riding a
    Bear* c. 1956
Grey stone
23.5 x 8.0 x 4.0 cm
The Winnipeg Art Gallery
Swinton Collection
Donated by the Women's Committee

Fig. 23.
Bear
Dorset culture
Alarnerk, Igloolik area
Ivory
15.7 cm (length)
National Museum of Man, National
    Museums of Canada, Ottawa

22

23

124.
Zacharie Ittimangnaq (1909-) m.
Man and Child with Bear and Cub c. 1974
Ivory, antler, and blacking
10.5 x 14.6 x 8.5 cm
Signed with syllabics
78/679

Fig. 24.
Man with Boy on His Shoulders
Dorset culture
Abverdjar, Igloolik area
Ivory
5.0 cm (height)
University Museum of Archaeology and
    Ethnology, Cambridge

CHARLIE NIPTAYUQ

Reaching back to preen itself the goose's head and neck create a closed arch over its body. Small in size, rounded and smooth, the ivory bird is appealingly tactile, its elegant white body accented only with the light touch of blacking to indicate the eyes.

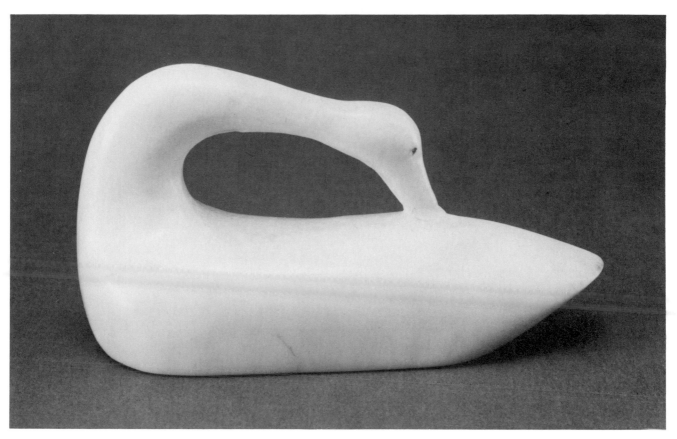

125.
Charlie Niptayuq (1943-) m.
Bird c. 1972
Ivory and blacking
3.5 x 5.8 x 2.4 cm
Unsigned
78/240

AGNES NULLUQ

Fig. 25.
Agnes Nulluq (1930-) f.
Pelly Bay
Shaman in Flight 1976
Ivory and bone
6.7 x 8.7 x 3.7 cm
Mr. and Mrs. Frits A. Begemann, Toronto

All three of these works by Agnes Nulluq (Nos. 126-128) are characterized by a certain subtlety of added embellishment – bird heads grow
from the woman's shoulders, knobs on the skull base become human
heads, and a bas-relief bird emerges from the bone base for the five owls.
In each case the added motif takes advantage of the natural shape in the
medium, gently emerging from the background area.

This ability of Nulluq's to combine forms, to have one motif merge
with another, is particularly evident in her sculpture *Shaman in Flight* (fig.
25). Here the bird and human forms are ingeniously fused into one; not
only are the shaman's arms and legs united with the bird's wings, but
both human and bird features make up the facial area.

While this fusion of shaman and bird, like Tookoome's animal/human
in his print *The World of Man and the World of Animals Come Together in
the Shaman* (No. 27), signifies deeper shamanic characteristics, the bird
and head motifs in the three Klamer sculptures seem to be more visually
oriented, as though the artist just wanted to further enrich the image.
Certainly the additional bird on the base of the *Five Owls* (No. 127) is
simply complementary to the bird subject matter. Perhaps in the other
two works the human faces on the base (No. 126) represent spirits and
the bird heads on the woman's shoulders (No. 128) relate to traditional
legends in which women turn into birds and fly away from their
husbands, but it seems more likely that they are just visual embellishments.

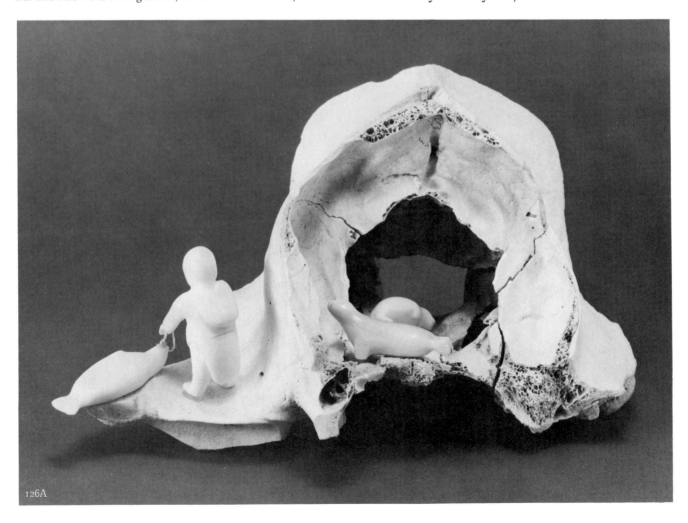

126A

127.
Agnes Nulluq (1930-) f.
Five Owls on Base c. 1973
Bone, ivory, and blacking
8.4 x 7.9 x 6.5 cm
Signed with syllabics
78/415

126.
Agnes Nulluq (1930-) f.
Woman and Seals on Base with Carved Heads
    1973
Bone, ivory, and sinew
10.3 x 19.8 x 12.6 cm
Signed with syllabics and dated
78/191

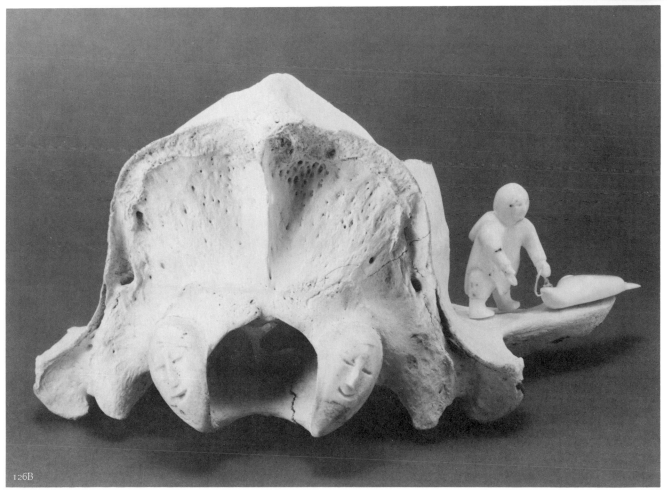

126B

128.
Agnes Nulluq (1930-) f.
*Woman with Bird Heads on Shoulders; Boy
    with Whip* c. 1974
Antler, hide, and sinew
16.5 x 7.0 x 15.8 cm
Unsigned
78/187

EMILY PANGNERK

In addition to the interesting combination of media here, and the striking use of the different coloured areas of the antler in the two figures' bodies, the subject matter in this sculpture is most intriguing (No. 129).

Certainly the figure in the foreground looks like a shaman in flight; he has protruding shamanic teeth and a body positioned as though for flight through the air or, perhaps, a dive to the lower regions. His placement on the ground immediately in front of the couple in their domestic setting with lamp and hide blanket could seem to be somewhat incongruous but for the fact that shamanic performances usually took place inside the small Eskimo dwelling. Special, large igloos might be built for group drum dances and séances, but often, especially when treating one individual, the shaman performed in the home of his client or patient. Most likely, then, these figures are all participants in a séance. The woman, her mouth open, bends slightly forward – perhaps she is chanting. The man, for his part, holds an unidentified object in his hand; is it, like in shamanic representations, a knife or some other implement of particular significance? Whatever the couple are doing, their role is a supporting one to the shamanic transformation in the foreground.

129.
Emily Pangnerk (1943-) f.
Séance c. 1973
Antler, caribou hide with hair, grey stone, ivory, and baleen
8.5 x 10.2 x 13.8 cm
Unsigned
78/427

DOMINIQUE TUNGILIK

People like the traditional Eskimos whose livelihood depends on the animals they hunt have a profound knowledge of, and respect for, their prey. Animals are hunted, not for sport, but in order to live. In the Arctic, the polar bear in particular was recognized as a dangerous opponent, but each animal had its talents and strong points in the chase, whether as the pursued or the pursuer. Man was only one of the hunters in the north; many animals, humans included, depended on the others for survival.

As the other pieces included in this section illustrate, ivory and bone are more commonly used by the Pelly Bay carvers than stone for making their sculptures. The stone used in this work is quite hard and has been only lightly detailed in the facial areas and on the seal's flippers. Nevertheless the carver has effectively modelled the stone to indicate the bones and musculature of his subjects.

130.
Dominique Tungilik (1920-) m.
Bear with Seal c. 1973
Grey stone and whitening
6.8 x 15.4 x 6.8 cm
Unsigned
78/634

MARTHA TUNNUK

While seals bask on top of an ice floe, a whale swims through the water nearby. Exquisitely carved themselves, the animals – done in ivory and contrasting black stone – are arranged in a topographical setting that utilizes the natural shape of the antler, whose smooth surface is embellished with complementary incised detailing.

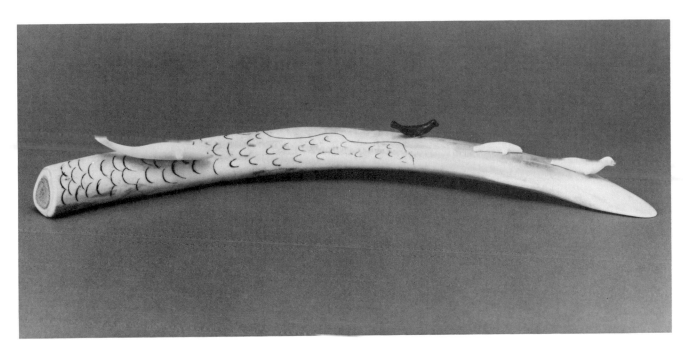

131.
Attributed to
Martha Tunnuk (1913-) f.
Whale and Seals on Base c. 1972
Antler, ivory, black stone, and blacking
2.9 X 22.5 X 8.1 cm
Unsigned
78/419

DAVIDIALUK ALASUA AMITUK

This early Davidialuk print gives little indication of what the artist's subsequent graphic work would be like. Atypical both in subject matter and in treatment, the 1961 *Owl on Kamotik* is much more restrained, much more static, and much narrower in focus than Davidialuk's later prints.

In this stonecut a large, lumpish owl sits on a disproportionately small sled. Its wing and feather structure and the sled's crossbars are defined with contrasting white linear markings, its eyes and beak by unprinted white areas. The two types of markings used for the bird's feathers – the U-shape and the longer lozenge shape – are similar to the incised markings on some of Davidialuk's carvings of birds. The owl's eyes, made up of several concentric circles, are not unlike those found in later sculpture and prints. Yet in other respects the owl heavily resting on his tiny *kamotik* is not typical.

Already in the 1962 Povungnituk graphic collection released a year later, Davidialuk's prints show a tremendous difference in style; considerable action transpires – a hunter falls out of his kayak, birds fly through the air, and birds and whales move through the rippling water. These activities are presented in appropriately dynamic graphic technique – utilizing multiple parallel lines, contrasting white and dark areas, and busy hatch marks. The scenes are full of life just as Davidialuk's later work would be.

Approximately ninety prints were released during Davidialuk's lifetime and in several posthumous collections. In these prints, as well as in his carvings and drawings, Davidialuk portrayed such subjects as shamans (fig. 3, p. 62), legends, stories, northern lights, hunting scenes, and various animals. Owls, for example, appear in several prints from 1976, but they differ from the one in this 1961 print in that they are more accurately portrayed and appear in a naturalistic setting, that is, nesting on the ground and flying through the air. Davidialuk does represent some unusual creatures in his work such as the legendary Kajjutaijuk, a monster with an enormous head resting on two stumpy legs, but his portrayals are consistent with story, legend, or natural fact, thus making our huge owl on a tiny sled incongruous.

It is for his many illustrations of traditional legends and stories as well as documentation of events that occurred in the course of his own life that Davidialuk is best known. Not only did he remember stories of the old ways, he recounted them to his spellbound northern audiences and depicted them for collectors in the south. His many legendary and narrative works record and keep alive a wealth of traditional and historical material.

132.
Davidialuk Alasua Amituk (1910-1976) m.
Owl on Kamotik 1961
Stonecut 22/60
61.3 x 46.1 cm
78/376

Among the techniques tried in the early printmaking experiments in Povungnituk was printing from a fibreglass plate cast in wax. This procedure, described in the exhibition catalogue *Things Made by Inuit* (Myers, p. 176), was not used again after these 1961 attempts.

> Wax is poured into a tray, possibly of wood, to a depth of about two inches. This, when hardened, forms a wax block into which lines are carved. A resin, probably fibreglass although it may have been epoxy, is poured into these lines and allowed to harden. The block can be reinforced with a fibreglass mat covering the surface and being brushed into the plate. After hardening, the plate is lifted out of the wax and filed level to become a printing surface.

In this technique the artist cuts his design into wax rather than stone. Although the printing stones used in the north are generally quite soft and can be cut with a sharp knife, working in wax would seem to have been even easier, allowing greater flexibility and finer definition in the cutting. And certainly in his rendering of *Family of Bird Hunters*, Syollie has incorporated considerable linear detailing such as footprints in the snow, and thin lines for bow strings. Yet in comparison with Syollie's later work this print is quite simple.

Since 1962 Syollie has produced approximately forty prints; all, but one stonecut and stencil, have been stonecuts. In making these prints Syollie cuts his stone block into complex designs; some are so complicated in perspective and motif as to be confusing, others showing sensitively etched, laboriously detailed birds.

Syollie, younger brother of the late Davidialuk, now lives in Great Whale River with his second wife. He continues to make prints on periodic visits to Povungnituk.

133.
Syollie Amituk (1932-) m.
Family of Bird Hunters 1961
Printed from a fibreglass plate cast in
    wax 38/60
31.2 x 45.8 cm
78/374

KANAYOOK AYAGUTAINAK

As a young man, not yet twenty, Kanayook was one of the original group of people to begin printmaking in Povungnituk in 1961. Since then he has continued producing prints, doing stone cutting and printing, and lately some stencil. Son of the well-known artist Ayagutainak, Kanayook also makes sculpture. In addition to his own work Kanayook has acted as manager of the Povungnituk printshop for a number of years.

In this early stonecut (signed with one of his other names Tukala) Kanayook portrays a striding polar bear, the texture of his fur indicated by the many short linear incisions in the stone that would have taken some time and effort to accomplish. Quite bold and assertive, this bear is not characteristic of Kanayook's style. Later works show curving, bending forms — usually animals such as otters, fish, and birds, which often viewed from an aerial vantage point, flow and intersect over the surface of the paper.

134.
Kanayook Ayagutainak (1942-) m.
Bear 1961
Stonecut 6/70
46.1 x 61.4 cm
78/373

SACKAREASIE NAPATUK

Stencil was another of the printing techniques tried in the 1961 experiments in Povungnituk, but it was not used on a regular basis until the 1970s and then only intermittently.

Here Sackareasie has sensitively used the stencil printing technique to apply lighter and darker areas to his long-necked goose, thus distinguishing different parts of the body and achieving a certain degree of shading and modelling.

This and possibly one other uncatalogued print are the only graphics Sackareasie has done. He now lives in Akulivik.

135.
Sackareasie Napatuk (1928-) m.
Canada Goose 1961
Stencil 37/50
48.0 x 62.9 cm
78/372

MAGGIE SHEEGUAPIK

In addition to this uncatalogued print from 1961, Maggie Sheeguapik has produced stonecuts for only two Povungnituk print collections – one in 1965, four in 1966.

Already in this early work we can see her ability to effectively use the white unprinted areas in conjunction with the printed dark ones in order to indicate different features or the division between individual parts of the images, and, in later works, to suggest the modelling of a rounded human face. Unprinted areas in the print *A Couple Fishing* (No. 136) make contrasting trim for the figures' dark-coloured clothing while distinguishing the *kamiks* on their feet from the garments on their legs. The white space between could have separated the *kamiks* too far from their owners, but several factors carry our eye over the gap – the use of similar white spaces in other places where their role is more clearly defined, the narrowness of the gap between boot and leg (a width equalling other white areas on the parkas), and our visual expectations.

In later works Maggie Sheeguapik becomes even more adroit at utilizing these intersecting and contrasting white and dark areas to show such things as a bird's feathers and the division between its extremities and its body, a dark hide tied to a rack with unprinted lines of white lashing, a printed *ulu* held in a white area in front of a printed dark body, and black protruding areas like the cheeks, chin, and nose of a face against the white shallower areas. A similar use of printed and unprinted areas is evident in the work of Maggie's late husband, Juanisialuk, who was also a printmaker.

Although the figures of the couple in this print are shown in profile, their faces are a combination of profile and frontal that could be awkward but is not. The foreground also shows two simultaneous views – the fish under the ice and the tiny sled and figures on top. Near the couple are their miniature implements, the woman's *ulu* and the ice fishing equipment.

136.
Maggie Sheeguapik (1916-) f.
A Couple Fishing 1961
Printed from a fibreglass plate cast in
    wax 6/50
36.5 x 45.6 cm
78/375

JOE TALIRUNILI

Fig. 26.
Joe Talirunili (1899-1976) m.
Povungnituk
*The People Takatak, Kinuajuak and
Kanavalik* c. 1960-1970
Graphite, wax crayon, and felt-tip pen
46.0 x 61.1 cm
National Collection of Inuit Art,
Canadian Ethnology Service, National
Museum of Man, National Museums
of Canada, Ottawa

The text on the drawing reads:

The people Takatak, Kinuajuak, Kanavalik,
on land were wondering if the canoe was
carrying white people or Indians. They
were very scared because they never
expected a boat in July. They thought they
were near death when they heard someone
shouting to them from the boat. This is
what they heard:

"We're Eskimo, we're not Indians or white
people. We were caught in the ice but this
is the first time we have seen land since a
long time." Woman shouting is Aula.
(Myers, *Joe Talirunili*, p. 50)

Throughout his artistic career Joe carved and recarved migration boat scenes showing a traditional *umiak* full of people. The subject, inspired by an event in his infancy, was one that he came back to over and over again. Elements would change, sometimes there was a sail; sometimes there were standing figures as well as the seated ones; sometimes one of the people had a harpoon, other times a telescope; sometimes the prow of the boat had a name plaque comprised of his first name, Joe, in English, his surname, Talirunili, in syllabics; but always the *umiak* seems to be overflowing with people.

In the original episode that inspired these carvings, in fact, the *umiak* was so overcrowded with people and their belongings it was barely navigable. According to Johnny Pov in his memories of Joe (Myers, *Joe Talirunili*, p. 6), several travelling Inuit families became stranded on an ice pan after it broke away from the coast. Blown out to sea as the ice pan began to break into smaller and smaller pieces, the travellers, using the wood from their sleds and skins they had with them, made a makeshift *umiak* to carry them over the water back to the mainland. Crowded into their boat, the people, the young Joe in his mother's parka among them, finally reached safety. In later life, when carving this episode from his childhood, Joe would try to remember all the people who had been on the boat, and according to Marybelle Myers (*Joe Talirunili*, p. 4), the carvings would sometimes be accompanied by a scrap of paper listing as many of the survivors as he could recall at the time.

In addition to his migrations, Joe concentrated on owls, and human figures in his sculpture. The sculptures included here, then, give a good idea of his carving subjects and technique, although they are perhaps more polished than was always Joe's practice. In his carvings, Joe was not one to be overly fussy about details — black string is used for harpoon lines where another artist would have used sinew, and this black string or glue, or putty, or anything else to hand seems to have been used to tie and stick recalcitrant carvings back together. And then there are the wooden or plastic rifles and other equipment carried by his figures. But Joe's carving methods, whether slapdash, crude, or unsophisticated, did produce results, results as successful and vibrant as he himself seems to have achieved in his personal quixotic approach to life.

Joe was also a draughtsman and a printmaker, activities that were easier for this man with a permanently unhealed gun shot wound in his right arm. He was one of the first to be involved in the Povungnituk printmaking program, and there have been over seventy of his stonecuts released since 1962. In these prints as in his drawings (Myers, *Joe Talirunili*, pp. 51-61), Joe depicted scenes full of traditional activities, more migrations, people, and animals. Owls such as No. 138 appear everywhere in his graphics. Often annotated with descriptive text, the drawings, done with delicacy and great sensitivity, provide considerable historical detail about Inuit life in Joe's time.

137.
Joe Talirunili (1899-1976) m.
Migration c. 1976
Grey stone, wood, hide, and string
29.0 x 18.0 x 31.0 cm
Unsigned
78/185
See colour plate on page 27.

138.
Joe Talirunili (1899-1976) m.
Owl c. 1976
Grey stone
15.5 x 7.8 x 12.8 cm
Signed with Roman
78/193

139.
Joe Talirunili (1899-1976) m.
Woman with Seal c. 1976
Black stone, grey stone, and string
7.5 X 9.1 X 6.9 cm
Signed with Roman
78/194

140.
Joe Talirunili (1899-1976) m.
Hunter with Harpoon c. 1976
Grey stone, wood, and string
20.2 X 8.7 X 7.7 cm
Signed with Roman
78/720

PIERRE KARLIK

Inuit people and animals of the north cover the surface of this ivory walrus tusk, their interdependence and interrelationships reinforced by the integration and intertwining of forms over the surface.

Compositions of this nature are a popular means of working ivory tusks; the arrangement of the various human and animal forms fitting together within the confines of the tusk shape, and taking full advantage of the carveable surfaces of the ivory. The smoothness and size of the walrus tusk also provide surfaces suitable for incising, and many artists, particularly in Alaska, decorate the tusks with graphic scenes. But other artists, both in Alaska and Canada, seem to prefer a more sculptural approach, and walrus tusks, even narwhal tusks, are carved into three-dimensional compositions. Although carved tusks of this type are not as common in Canada as they are in Alaska, examples were collected in the early twentieth century in the Arctic Quebec/Labrador area. More recent examples come from areas like Chesterfield Inlet or Lake Harbour where the carvers have access to ivory and are accustomed to working with it.

Pierre Karlik was originally from Chesterfield Inlet and it was in the hospital there in the 1950s, where he spent five years suffering from polio, that he began carving.

The style and format of this carved tusk may have its origin in Karlik's early work at Chesterfield but other carvings done by him after his move to Rankin Inlet in 1961 indicate that the choice and positioning of figures here is not determined solely by the natural shape of the tusk. For one thing, Karlik's carvings done in stone also represent groupings of people and/or animals similar to those done by him on walrus and narwhal tusks. For another, Karlik has himself commented on some of his carvings, and his statements show him to be a sensitive and perceptive artist who observes and thoughtfully considers what goes on around him. For example, his 1976 carving entitled *Inuit Ublumi (Inuit Today)*, commissioned by the National Museum of Man in Ottawa, is a sculpture with an explicit message. The carving uses artistic symbols and overt signs to illustrate the dilemma of the contemporary Inuit who, as Karlik says in an accompanying written statement, "are no longer able to live their traditional lifestyle. . . . who are still unable to fit into white man's lifestyle." According to Karlik, his carvings of various species of arctic animals show their interdependent lifestyle; in our sculpture it would seem that the positioning of the human faces is related to visual concerns and to the slight margin humans have over the other animals in northern life.

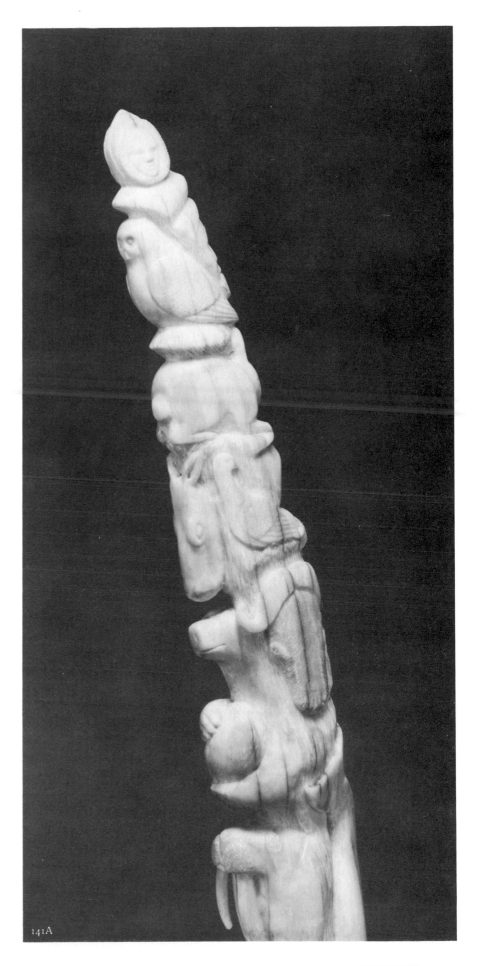

141A

141.
Pierre Karlik (1931-) m.
Carved Walrus Tusk c. 1974
Ivory and black stone
44.0 x 10.7 x 7.1 cm
Signed with syllabics and Roman
78/672

141B

141C

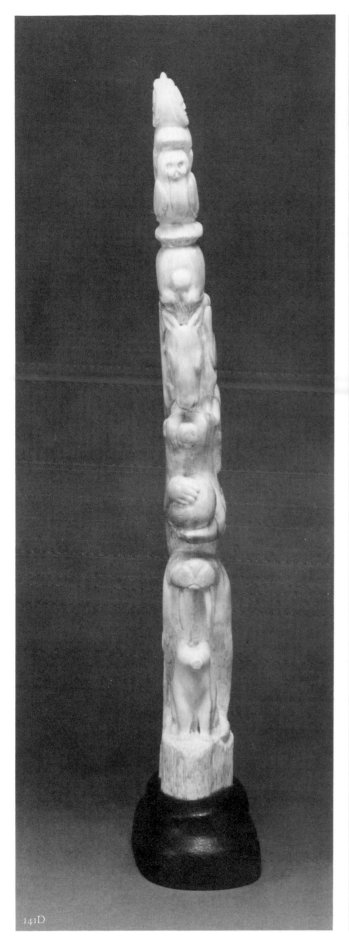

141D

141E

JOHN KAVIK

To say that Kavik concentrates on the human figure in his work would be accurate but inadequate. As the three sculptures illustrated here indicate, Kavik's treatment of his human subject is as wide ranging as Lachaulassie's treatment of his bird subject. But unlike Lachaulassie's birds that are often light-hearted, quirky, or humorous, many of Kavik's sculptural figures have an intensity and poignancy that is deeply moving.

While the mother in the sculpture *Mother and Child* (No. 143) clasps the child to her body in a typically warm and protective gesture, the relationship between the people in the carving of *Two Figures* (No. 142) is more difficult to determine. Here the positioning of the two people suggests that the large figure in front is being held by the person behind, as easily as a small child would be; yet the two people are virtually the same size. The faces of the two do seem to be differentiated – the features of the figure in front look younger and more filled out than the shrunken, perhaps toothless mouth, the pinched and wrinkled eyes, and the thin skin stretched over the high cheekbones of the figure behind. The slight bulge and typical line of a female parka flap suggest that the older figure is a woman. Is this perhaps a vision of the now fragile old woman holding her once portable child – now a grown man?

Nine sculptures by Kavik were included in the Masterworks exhibition (Canadian Eskimo Arts Council, *Sculpture/Inuit*, Nos. 102, 223, 284, 291, 322, 346, 359, 386, 397). There are single figures and double figures, one man carries a caribou, another does a somersaulting flip, there are mothers – even one shown as pregnant – with their children, a kneeling woman, a kneeling man, and one figure overshadowed by a schematic parka image. In other works Kavik shows great broad-shouldered primordial figures; in another the head of a figure wearing snow goggles (The Winnipeg Art Gallery, *The Zazelenchuk Collection of Eskimo Art*, Nos. 102, 103) like the man in our sculpture *Crouching Figure Wearing Snow Goggles* (No. 144).

Like Lachaulassie, Kavik creates his expressive images with very little surface articulation. His statements are direct and basic; the figures are achieved with gouges, incised lines, and some modelling and shaping. Arms, feet, knees, thighs, parka lines, parka hoods, and facial features are suggested, roughed in, or drilled out.

Human figures are the most prevalent subjects in Kavik's work, but he also carves animals and birds. Although he does not recall the *Bird* (No. 145) included here, it has been attributed to him on the basis of its style. In addition to carving, Kavik also made ceramics through the Rankin Inlet pottery program. Examples of his work in clay, in which human forms and faces and animals emerge from the sides of his pots, can be seen in Henrika Nagy's *Beaver* article ''Pottery in Keewatin'' (p. 64), in W. T. Larmour's *Keewatin Eskimo Ceramics '67* (p. 7) and the Winnipeg Art Gallery *Rankin Inlet* catalogue (No. 17).

Kavik, who was born in Gjoa Haven, lived in Baker Lake before settling in 1959 in Rankin Inlet where he still lives. His artistic career began when he was in his late sixties and the works included here were done when he was in his seventies.

142. Opposite
John Kavik (1897-) m.
Two Figures c. 1971
Dark grey stone
13.8 x 6.0 x 5.0 cm
Unsigned
78/721

143.
John Kavik (1897-   ) m.
Mother and Child c. 1973
Grey stone
12.5 X 11.0 X 5.0 cm
Unsigned
78/413

145.
Attributed to
John Kavik (1897-) m.
Bird c. 1973
Grey stone
7.5 x 17.8 x 7.9 cm
Unsigned
78/407

144.
John Kavik (1897-) m.
Crouching Figure Wearing Snow Goggles
   c. 1973
Grey stone
13.0 x 9.8 x 14.3 cm
Signed with syllabics
78/416

Fitted and nestled together over the surface of the stone, Tiktak's faces are evocative of the interpersonal relationships in traditional Inuit lifestyle, when members of the extended family were totally dependent upon themselves and the others in their small group. Each person, young or old, fulfilled a function – the men hunted, the women sewed and prepared food, the old men made equipment, the old women helped with domestic chores, and the children learned by doing, so that one day they could in turn take care of their elders. And while everyone had their own area of expertise and responsibility, this was generally so time-consuming or specialized that they were dependent on others for the other things. The hunter, looking for game to feed and clothe his family, did not have time to also sew all his own clothing and footwear. Each person, then, had a contributory and dependent role.

Tiktak's concern with humanity is dominant in his work. There are groupings of human faces, single human figures, and single human faces; sometimes there are two figures or partial figures – many of them clearly a mother and child. Often in these, as in *Mother and Child* (No. 146), the body of the child seems to grow from that of the mother, the offspring a literal and symbolic by-product of the parent.

In his representations of the human being, Tiktak concentrated on the face of the figure to the point of sometimes excluding the body altogether. Even carvings of full figures emphasize the face rather than such features as clothing, hair, or articulated extremities. These faces, too, are done with little modelling and definition, a separate continuous scored or gouged out line indicates the eye and the side of the nose, resulting in some rounding of the cheek area. A single horizontal line becomes the mouth. In their sophisticated simplicity, Tiktak's carvings – with their emphasis on form, mass, and shape – speak to us of humanity, of human feelings, emotions, and needs.

146.
John Tiktak (1916-1981) m.
Mother and Child c. 1971
Grey stone
15.0 X 6.0 X 7.5 cm
Signed with syllabics
78/234

147A

147.
John Tiktak (1916-1981) m.
Faces c. 1973
Grey stone
28.5 x 24.3 x 14.0 cm
Signed with syllabics
78/402

147B

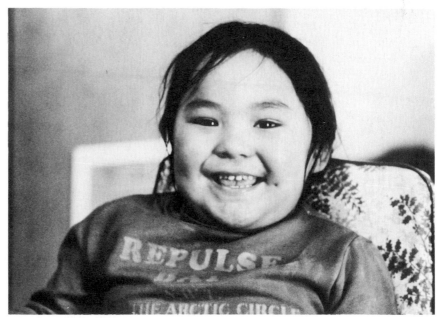

Like the hard grey stone used farther down the coast in Rankin Inlet and Eskimo Point, the stone in these two sculptures (common in 1960s sculptures from Repulse Bay) does not lend itself to easy carving, detailing, or glossy polishing. Works in such material tend to use the shape and attitude of the figure rather than details to convey the essence of the subject. The "bearness" of the striding polar bear (No. 148) is immediately conveyed to us in spite of his stiff, stilt-like legs.

The straight-on frontal portrait of the woman (No. 149), too, could be rather stiff, but its potentially austere air is softened by the linear detailing of her hair and clothing and, more important, by the slight angling of her body to one side counterbalanced by the slight tilt of her head in the opposite direction.

Single standing figures like No. 149, posed as though for a camera snapshot, are not unusual in Repulse Bay sculpture (see fig. 27, p. 234), and the simplicity of the subject is a real contrast to the more typical complex composite scenes. Nevertheless these lone figures appeal directly to us in their simplicity and earnestness.

148.
Rosa Arnarudluk (1914-) f.
Bear c. 1966
Grey stone
10.5 x 17.6 x 6.0 cm
Unsigned
78/210

149A

149B

149.
Rosa Arnarudluk (1914-) f.
Woman c. 1966
Grey stone
18.7 x 8.5 x 5.7 cm
Unsigned
78/211

MARIANO AUPILARJUK

The subject matter in both of these carvings (Nos. 150-151) is somewhat unusual. The representation of spirits and shamans is not common in Repulse Bay sculpture, and the presentation of an overt social statement is rare in art work from any part of the Canadian Arctic.

For all the cultural upheaval the Inuit have experienced, particularly within the last twenty to thirty years, a surprisingly small number of art works recognize this change and even fewer comment upon it. Artists like Pudlo who regularly represent airplanes, Etidlooie who drew views of houses and buildings in downtown Cape Dorset, and Oonark who may use a snowmobile motif in her wall hangings or drawings are far outnumbered by the artists who continue to illustrate traditional activities and settings. But whatever their subject, both these types of work generally indicate no value judgment on circumstances in the north; they simply represent it.

Only a few people have used their art work as a forum for social commentary. In some cases the work can visually express the distress and concern, other times an explanatory text is included. A recent carving by Ovilu Toonoo of Cape Dorset of two figures (unpublished) shows a white man bottle-feeding alcohol to an Inuk. Eli Sallualuk, in one of his carvings (unpublished), demonstrates and explains in Inuktitut about the effects of imported venereal disease. Thomassie Kudluk of Payne Bay speaks out from the north through a scene incised on the underside of one of his carvings (Myers, *Things Made by Inuit*, p. 47). The text accompanying the illustration of an Inuk on an elevated arch of land reads: "The man addresses the country of Canada with outstretched arms, saying to the white people: 'I am higher than all governments, therefore I deserve to be heard!'"

Not as visually explicit or pointed in its commentary as these sculptures, the Aupilarjuk carving *Grasp Tight the Old Ways* (No. 150) still makes an urgent plea for the preservation of Inuit cultural heritage. In this sculpture, the phrase used for the title is incised on the top of the base between the two people. The Inuktitut text which expresses the idea of holding onto, of not letting go of the old customs or culture explains the gestures of the two figures. Sculpturally unremarkable, these figures are done with much less finesse than Aupilarjuk demonstrates in other sculptures illustrated in several publications (Canadian Eskimo Arts Council, *Sculpture/Inuit*, No. 327; The Winnipeg Art Gallery, *Repulse Bay*, Nos. 24-26). Obviously here the message is more important than the image.

In the other sculpture included here (No. 151) Aupilarjuk represents a standing human figure with animal paws and ears. This may represent a spirit but it seems more likely that a shamanic transformation has transpired. Although only a small clue, the representation of circular o-shaped mouths is connected with shamanism, probably associated with life-giving breath. Also of interest is the ornament on the figure's head. Headdresses of various kinds can sometimes be seen in representations of shamans (Blodgett, *The Coming and Going of the Shaman*, Nos. 120, 168).

Examination of art works from different communities indicates that the prevalence of shamanic subjects varies from place to place. The artists of Repulse Bay and Inukjuak, for example, tend not to represent subjects related to shamanism; instead, they specialize in what might be considered to be less controversial subjects such as people animals, and

150.
Mariano Aupilarjuk (1923-) m.
Grasp Tight the Old Ways c. 1973
Green stone, ivory, antler, and blacking
7.1 x 6.6. x 5.8 cm
Signed with syllabics
78/396

everyday activities. It would appear that this characteristic can be traced back to previous association with white people, and these outsiders' reaction to Inuit customs. Even before conversion to Christianity forced shamanism underground, the scorn, derision, and superior attitude of outsiders persuaded certain Inuit groups to keep shamanic practices and religious beliefs to themselves.

Many of Aupilarjuk's carvings represent the everyday – birds, whales swimming through waves, or a hunter pursuing his prey. His sculpture *Multiple Image* in the Masterworks exhibition (Canadian Eskimo Arts Council, *Sculpture/Inuit*, No. 327; also reproduced in the Winnipeg Art Gallery, *Repulse Bay*, No. 25), however, seems to operate on a deeper level, with the possibility of several interpretations. The sculpture represents a human face, bears, and a walrus. The conjunction of the bear and the human head, and the bear with the walrus may be related to shamanism and to a symbolic union between the walrus and the bear. This sculpture and the two included here indicate that Aupilarjuk, in addition to his representations of everyday subjects, is prepared to contend with religious and social issues in his work.

151.
Mariano Aupilarjuk (1923-) m.
Shaman c. 1973
Ivory, green stone, brown stone, antler,
  and graphite
11.0 X 9.4 X 5.4 cm
Signed with syllabics
78/398

BERNADETTE IGUPTAQ

Sculptural compositions with one or more figures arranged on a base is a very popular format in Repulse Bay. The stone, bone, or antler base helps set the scene for activities on land, in the air, or in the water. Sometimes, in fact, the configuration of the base is used to indicate several levels of terrain or activity – the hunter at a seal hole stands on a base area raised up to provide us with a view of the seal in the water beneath, a happy bear stands over his seal dinner-to-be on an ice floe while his two envious companions swimming in the water below peer over the edge, birds pegged high above the base fly overhead while a family standing near their tent on land wave goodbye to their friends departing in a boat in the water below.

In the Iguptaq sculpture of the *Narwhal* (No. 152) his elevation on a peg above the base creates a sense of space and weightlessness compatible with swimming through the water. In the hunting scene (No. 153), some topographical variation is provided by the slight change in elevation between the walrus's level and where the man stands.

Both scenes are very finely carved with minute details such as contrasting inset eyes; thin, delicate narwhal tusk and flukes; and the small harpoon with realistic, braided sinew line. The realism of the hunting scene in particular would seem to bespeak a knowledgeable hunter as the originator rather than a woman. In Cape Dorset graphics, for example, it is often the male hunters (like Kananginak) who depict the more naturalistic birds, animals, and hunting activities while the women (like Pitseolak and Kenojuak) concentrate on domestic scenes and visual effects. When the women do show hunting or wildlife, the approach seems oriented more to esthetics than realism. Certainly many of the changes made to Kenojuak drawings over the years by the men printing them were intended, as they explain, to create more naturalistic representations.

As the proportion of male to female carvers included in this book indicates, women in Repulse Bay take an active part in the community's sculptural work. And while the women seem to portray more domestic scenes, such as tableaus of hide scraping and cleaning, than the men, they also depict a variety of hunting scenes comparable in format, detailing, realism, and quality to those made by their male counterparts. One has only to compare the carving of *Man in Kayak Hunting Caribou* by Madeleine Isserkut (The Winnipeg Art Gallery, *Repulse Bay*, No. 37) to a sculpture of the same title by Mariano Aupilarjuk (The Winnipeg Art Gallery, *Repulse Bay*, No. 24) or Suzanne Tiyiteark's *Man Harpooning Seal* (The Winnipeg Art Gallery, *Repulse Bay*, No. 82) to Mark Tungilik's *Men Fishing* (The Winnipeg Art Gallery, *Repulse Bay*, No. 86) to see the similarities.

In addition to this hunting scene and others such as her *Man and Dog at Seal Hole* (The Winnipeg Art Gallery, *Repulse Bay*, No. 29), Bernadette Iguptaq has carved a variety of other subjects, sometimes working in stone rather than ivory. Her *Drum Dancer* was included in the Masterworks exhibition (Canadian Eskimo Arts Council, *Sculpture/Inuit*, No. 222), and the Winnipeg Art Gallery collection includes carvings of birds, animals, group and domestic scenes. Her marvelous version of the *Legend of Lumaiyo* is illustrated in the Agnes Etherington Art Centre's catalogue *Inuit Art of the 1970's* (No. 14).

152.
Bernadette Iguptaq (1931-) f.
Narwhal 1974
Ivory, black stone, bone, and blacking
8.5 x 15.5 x 3.3 cm
Signed with syllabics and dated
78/196

153.
Bernadette Iguptaq (1931-) f.
Man Harpooning Walrus c. 1974
Dark green-black stone, ivory, sinew,
    and baleen
7.5 x 9.5 x 6.2 cm
Signed with syllabics
78/195

Fig. 27.
Madeleine Isserkut (1928-) f.
Repulse Bay
Man
Beige stone
11.5 x 3.8 x 3.2 cm
The Jerry Twomey Collection, The
    Winnipeg Art Gallery – with apprecia-
    tion to the Province of Manitoba and
    the Government of Canada

Working with his snow knife inside the rising structure, the man builds up the igloo walls with blocks of wind-packed snow while the woman uses her snow shovel to pack and fill the cracks.

Everyday, domestic scenes are typical of Repulse Bay sculpture: small-scale, intimate scenes that give us delightful insight into Inuit life. While single walrus tusks of ivory left intact can be worked into carvings of some size (No. 141), the Repulse Bay sculptors tend to use smaller pieces of ivory to create composite scenes on a stone or bone base. Constructions of this nature enable the carvers, in a sculptural format, to build up complex compositions that in a printmaking community might find expression on paper. Without a graphics program, the Repulse Bay artists still can depict such things as interaction between subjects, passage of time, or simultaneous activities within one carving. The modest proportions of these scenes seem perfectly in keeping with their unassuming, even folksy style.

An important aspect of the Repulse Bay scenes is the small detailing such as the incised lines in the igloo wall in No. 154 showing the up-wardly spiralling snow blocks and the accurately fashioned implements. The proportions, such as the relation between the people and their too-small igloo, are adjusted as need be. These changes are made, however, in keeping with the physical limitations of the size of the ivory and the scene itself. Although Repulse Bay carvers may exercise some artistic license, their carvings tend to be explicit and straightforward, showing things as they are. Their approach can be contrasted to the minimal style characteristic of carvings by many Rankin Inlet and Eskimo Point sculptors, and to the exaggeration of the expressive, imaginative carvings from Cape Dorset.

Madeleine Isserkut is a prolific carver whose works have been well documented. Illustrations of her sculptures in the Canadian Eskimo Arts Council's *Sculpture/Inuit* catalogue (Nos. 220, 305), the Canadian Guild of Crafts Quebec book edited by Virginia Watt (Nos. 55, 118, 275, 284), Nelda Swinton's *Inuit Sea Goddess* catalogue (No. 41), and the Winnipeg Art Gallery's *Repulse Bay* catalogue (Nos. 33-40) give some idea of her carving media, subjects, and style. Able to work with equal ease in stone or ivory, she portrays hunting and domestic scenes including kayakers pursuing caribou or bears, igloo building, animals with elaborate miniature horns, and birds with paper-thin and curved flapping wings. There is also a marvelous, stiffly correct, and completely out-of-his-element white man dressed in southern attire (fig. 27) who makes an interesting comparison with Rosa Arnarudluk's *Woman* (No. 149). Madeleine Isserkut's *Drum Dancer* and one by Jean Mapsalak, also of Repulse Bay, were reproduced on a seventeen-cent stamp released in 1979.

154.
Madeleine Isserkut (1928-) f.
Building an Igloo c. 1974
Bone, ivory, wood, and sinew
7.3 X 11.5 X 9.2 cm
Signed with syllabics
78/683

ALEXINA PANANA NAKTAR

While insetting ivory or contrasting coloured stone faces into carved stone figures was quite popular in the Inukjuak area in the 1950s, the practice is not a common one in Repulse Bay or anywhere else in the Canadian Arctic. Even more remarkable about this carving is that the insetting is done with antler into whalebone. Whalebone sculptures may have detailing in antler, but this usually consists of small accents such as eyes, or teeth, or the horns that would have been antler in the original animal.

Antler seems a strange choice for the small insets here; it is difficult enough to work on a larger scale, and file marks are still evident here. Yet the artist has managed to fashion appropriately tiny features for the baby and the more mature ones of the mother whose eyes are softly highlighted with graphite. Forming a most effective frame for the two faces is the dark-coloured whalebone. Here, the artist has made excellent use of the colour variations naturally occurring in whalebone; the shift from lighter to darker bone is coordinated with the neck area so that the faces of the mother and child are each set into a contrasting background. This dark area, looking alternately like hair or a parka hood trimmed with fur, accents the two faces rising above the woman's columnar body.

155.
Alexina Panana Naktar (1943-) f.
Mother and Child c. 1970
Whalebone, antler, and graphite
22.5 X 10.8 X 9.7 cm
Unsigned
78/202
See colour plate on page 23.

ROSALIE OOKANGOK

Her aquatic tail gracefully flowing out in front of her, the ivory sea goddess sits on a contrasting black stone base. While many representations of Taleelayo show her in her marine environment or emphasize her seagoing nature, here she is shown resting upright out on land. Although the position is an unusual one, it is virtually identical to that of a sea goddess in a carving by Madeleine Isserkut, dated several years later, illustrated in the catalogue *The Inuit Sea Goddess* (Nelda Swinton, No. 41).

Our sea goddess, instead of clasping her arms to her waist, holds them out in front of her thus making them more prominent. The fingerless stumps so displayed reflect accurately an episode in the Taleelayo legend where the goddess-to-be is thrown overboard from her father's boat in his attempt to save himself from the raging storm caused by Taleelayo's rejected and furious bird husband. Each time as she tries to grasp hold of the gunwale, her father chops off her fingers, joint by joint, until her fingerless hands are unable to support her and she falls back into the sea. Her finger joints become various sea animals and she their protectress.

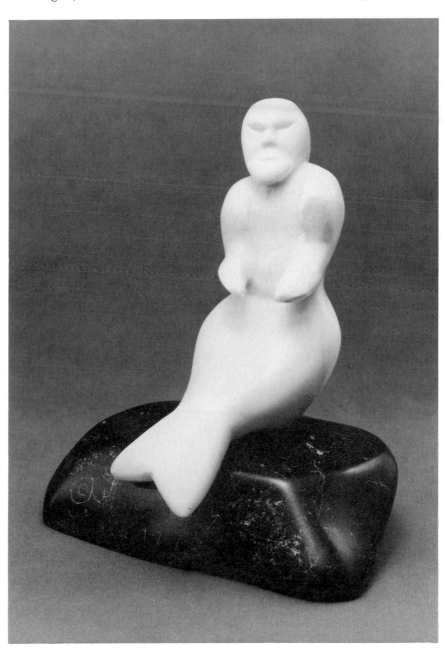

156.
Rosalie Ookangok (1935-) f.
Sea Goddess 1973
Black stone, ivory, and antler
11.0 x 9.3 x 9.2 cm
Signed with syllabics and dated
78/390

KAROO ASHEVAK

In the short span of an artistic career that lasted for only about four years before his death in 1974, Karoo Ashevak established himself as one of the major contemporary Inuit sculptors. Working primarily in whalebone, using stone, antler, ivory, and baleen mostly for insets and embellishments, Karoo carved spirits, shamans (fig. 4, p. 62), walruses, bears, birds, human figures and heads. These works are characterized by a lively sense of animation, religious undertones, humour and an assured and accomplished sculptural genius.

While Karoo might take advantage of the unusual natural shapes and colours in whalebone, he generally started a carving with a particular subject in mind, having searched for an appropriate piece of bone for his forthcoming sculpture. Working with the bone, he utilized naturally occurring configurations and then added parts or bases, set in eyes, and incised arms, wings, or parka trim. The *Head* (No. 158) here has an ivory tongue, while one of the two heads in the *Two-Headed Figure* (No. 157) has little ivory pebbles in his mouth, perhaps representing food (as similar objects do in other sculptures) so that the figure need never be hungry as Inuit so often used to be. Perhaps they are just additional component parts, since Karoo loved to play with his creations, building them up, taking them apart, and putting them back together again.

Karoo, featured in a one-man exhibition at the Winnipeg Art Gallery an 1977 (Blodgett, *Karoo Ashevak*), specialized in the fine finishing details which are so characteristic of his technique. The eyes in both works here are done with typical insets made up of several rings of contrasting materials. In later works the eyes become even more complex and more unusual; they grow large or small, wander over the facial area, or protrude and peer backward over the figure's shoulder. Later works, in general, show an increased complexity and bizarreness that is indicated by the double heads in this early *Two-Headed Figure*.

158.
Karoo Ashevak (1940-1974) m.
Head c. 1972
Whalebone, antler, and baleen
18.0 X 10.8 X 10.0 cm
Signed with syllabics
78/737

157. Opposite
Karoo Ashevak (1940-1974) m.
Two-Headed Figure 1971
Whalebone, ivory, and stone
65.3 X 31.5 X 16.5 cm
Signed with syllabics
78/690

MUGUALUK PADLAYAT

Although the smaller figure in No. 159 looks more like a miniature adult (suggesting the possible interpretation that this carving illustrates the well-known Arctic Quebec legend of the Inuk and the giant), it is more likely that what is represented is an intimate, playful scene of a father and his son. Human figures are a popular subject in Sugluk sculpture, and collections such as the Winnipeg Art Gallery include a number of carvings representing men, women, and children standing and seated singly or grouped together. These figures may be engaged in domestic activities, but often they are shown just at ease together, as though simply enjoying each other's company. The subject of one piece in particular by an unknown artist showing a *Mother and Child at Play* (fig. 28) can be compared to this work by Mugualuk Padlayat.

Without other published examples of Mugualuk's sculpture it is not possible to discuss this carving within the context of his work. The type of hard, grey stone and his treatment of it, however, suggest that the piece dates to the late 1950s, possibly early 1960s. Sugluk carvers at this time tended to use less inset ivory decoration than their fellow artists in Inukjuak, and their harder stone precluded the type of complex incised linear decoration favoured by some Povungnituk sculptors. Although they did do some fine incising to represent such things as hair, the Sugluk carvers extensively used the broader pleats, creases, and folds of clothing garments as though trying to somehow break the monotony of the wide expanse of flat, grey stone. This technique, employed so liberally here by Mugualuk can also be seen in the woman's skirt in the *Mother and Child at Play* (fig. 28) and to a lesser degree in a sculpture of a *Mother and Child* by Mugualuk's son Isaaci Padlayat included in the Masterworks exhibition (Canadian Eskimo Arts Council, *Sculpture/Inuit*, No. 289).

The creases and folds in Mugualuk's sculpture give a realistic representation of the way the clothing – one is tempted to say drapery – of the figures actually falls, while the direction of the creases helps distinguish one piece of clothing from another – the horizontal lines of the man's sagging *kamiks*, the diagonal lines of his pants pulled out by the protruding buttocks, and the opposite diagonal of the parka lines pulled away from his back to the extended arms. In addition, these representational lines, at least on the side of the sculpture illustrated (No. 159), symbolically reinforce the movement of the action taking place, starting with the more static horizontal lines of the man's boots and then spiralling up with the diagonals to the upper part of the sculpture. The curved lines of the boy's parka, as well as his higher position, help to balance the sculpture, offsetting the greater weight of the father on the right. At the same time, the diagonal creases of the boy's parka form an arc with the folds at the bottom of his father's parka. This diagonal line, interrupted but not broken by the boy's plain pants, unites the two figures and reinforces their relationship.

Fig. 28.
Artist Unknown
Sugluk
Mother and Child at Play 1955
Grey stone
22.2 x 11.4 x 10.8 cm
The Winnipeg Art Gallery
Swinton Collection
Donated by the Women's Committee

159.
Mugualuk Padlayat (1906-1968) m.
Father and Son 1950s
Grey stone
28.0 x 16.2 x 12.7 cm
Signed with disc number
78/732

BOBBY QUPPAAPIK TARKIRK

Trees may not grow in the Arctic but they do appear in some Inuit graphics and sculpture. The Montreal Museum of Fine Arts has in its collection a tree with leaves on the branches and a bird on top – all made from pieces of ivory (George Swinton, *Sculpture of the Eskimo*, No. 171). This somewhat schematic tree, which is supported on a three-pronged base, dates to about 1900 and comes from Moose Factory, presumably made by an Inuk patient at the hospital there. Later carvings of trees, such as one by Shoovegar of Frobisher Bay (Blodgett, *Looking South*, No. 23) and the one included here (No. 160), utilize caribou antler for the tree itself. The branching antler, often anchored to a stone base, provides appropriate perches for the carved stone birds.

The stone used in this sculpture is readily identifiable as coming from the Cape Dorset area, and the original tag gave Cape Dorset as the community of origin. When inquiries were made in Cape Dorset, however, everyone agreed that the piece had not been made by a Dorset artist. Further research established that the tree was made by a man from Sugluk known as Bobby who had been in Cape Dorset in the late 1960s.

Travel between Cape Dorset and Sugluk is more frequent than is perhaps realized from our distance down south. Many famous Cape Dorset artists such as Lucy, Pitseolak, Kiakshuk, and Kenojuak either moved to south Baffin as children or their families originally migrated there from Arctic Quebec. Visitors from Sugluk are common in Cape Dorset; in summer their boats anchored offshore indicate that someone in the community has visiting friends or relatives from across Hudson Strait.

According to different reports, Bobby came to Cape Dorset for a bigger market for his carvings (Raine, "The Miniatures of Bobby Takrik," p. 16) or because of his concern about the impending provincial takeover of functions that had been up to then administered by the federal government (Roberts, *The Inuit Artists of Sugluk, P.Q.*, p. 55). Whatever the reason for his move, Bobby settled in Cape Dorset for several years and continued to carve; he returned to Sugluk in the early 1970s.

Even before he came to Dorset Bobby was recognized for his carving of miniature sculptures. He had established a reputation both in Sugluk and then in Povungnituk where he lived for several years in the mid-1960s. In 1971, his work was featured in an article by David Raine in *The Beaver* magazine.

Bobby's work on miniatures has certainly influenced this carving of *Birds on Tree*, as he deals with smaller elements joined together to make a composite whole. The little birds, each one different and each perched on its own branch, are carefully fashioned and embellished with incised lines. Although one side of the whitish antler has been left blank, the other has been decorated with several incised and blackened motifs – a walrus, a successful seal hunter, and a human whose spreading hair flows up the antler branches.

160A

160.
Bobby Quppaapik Tarkirk (1934-) m.
Sugluk (and Cape Dorset)
Birds on Tree c. 1969
Antler, green stone, wood, metal, and
   blacking
51.5 x 45.4 x 20.8 cm
Unsigned
78/230

160B

The provenance of these three ivories (Nos. 161-163) purchased by the Klamers in the late 1960s is unknown. While the type of stone used in contemporary carvings often helps to pinpoint the community of origin, and while antler and whalebone works tend to come from certain areas, ivory is temporally and geographically more widespread. Most communities at one time or another, especially in the years before the 1950s when stone work was encouraged, have used ivory extensively.

Nor does the carving style in these works definitely point to a particular place of origin. Contemporary ivories may exhibit characteristics common to the sculptural style of their community of origin, but ivories from the early part of the 1900s seem to be less specific in style, probably primarily because the data are so incomplete that we have been unable to firmly establish the stylistic characteristics of certain areas, but also because the ivory works are less distinctive in size, treatment, and subject matter than later carvings in other media.

The size, formats (such as the arrangement on a base), and subject matter of all three of these ivories are typical of carvings made for sale rather than for the Inuit's own use. This and the fact that the woman of the *Couple* (No. 162) wears a modern skirt suggest a date of post 1900. The *Man in Kayak* (No. 161) and the *Bear* (No. 163) especially could even be contemporary works, possibly from Pelly Bay. The format of the *Couple* and the use of a wooden base for the ivory figures seem more characteristic of works from the 1930s from areas such as Pangnirtung, Lake Harbour, and south Baffin Island, or the western Canadian Arctic. Whalers and other outsiders who regularly purchased souvenir carvings frequented these places, and wood was available through barter, wreckage, or, in the west, nearby trees.

The *Bear* and the *Man in Kayak* exhibit particularly fine detailing work. The *Bear* has incised lines filled with blacking to indicate his eyes, claws, and hairy snout. The *Man in Kayak* is shown with a full complement of kayak hunting equipment which is pegged to his vessel with great care. This approach – the exact replica model – was a popular type of carving during the early to mid-1900s.

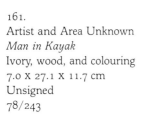

161.
Artist and Area Unknown
Man in Kayak
Ivory, wood, and colouring
7.0 X 27.1 X 11.7 cm
Unsigned
78/243

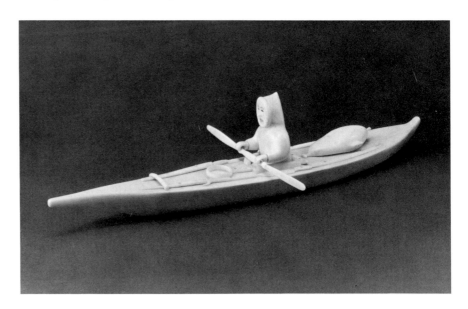

162.
Artist and Area Unknown
Couple
Ivory, wood, and blacking
12.5 x 12.8 x 4.0 cm
Unsigned
78/727

163.
Artist and Area Unknown
Bear
Ivory and blacking
7.0 x 12.7 x 4.0 cm
Unsigned
78/729

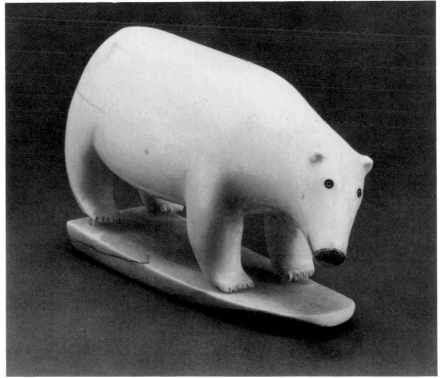

ARTIFACTS
by Henry B. Collins
Dorothy Jean Ray
James W. VanStone

Eskimos place considerable reliance on amulets or talismans which were worn or carried on the person and believed to bring good luck to a variety of endeavours. This ivory carving of unknown age may have been attached to a shaman's clothing, representing his affiliation with a specific supernatural helper.

J.W.VS.

164.
Attachment for Shaman's Clothing
Prehistoric
North American Arctic
Ivory
2.3 cm (height)
78/459

In no other class of objects, not even the elaborately decorated prehistoric harpoon heads, is the Eskimos' artistry and esthetic sense more clearly revealed than in the so-called winged objects. These ivory objects, carved in different but sequentially related forms and decorated with the designs characteristic of the Okvik, Old Bering Sea, and Punuk phases of prehistoric Alaskan Eskimo art, were apparently attached to the butt end of the harpoon shaft to act as a counterweight and balance for the heavy harpoon head and socket piece at the opposite (fore) end (Collins, *Archaeology of St. Lawrence Island, Alaska*, pp. 41-3, 87-9, 197-201; "Eskimo Cultures," cols. 5-7; "Eskimo Art," p. 8). The present example is of the Okvik (earliest) stage, probably from St. Lawrence Island. It has the short, stubby outer wings characteristic of Okvik. The incised decoration on the front or outer surface includes pairs of large circles suggestive of later Old Bering Sea art, but the form of the circles themselves (flat, rather than elevated) and the accompanying linear decoration (straight, double lines rather than curved lines) are typical of Okvik. The incised decoration on the opposite side is also Okvik, but with a new feature 13– a human face carved in low relief inside a large oval or circular panel. In other examples of Okvik and Old Bering Sea winged objects the decorative elements are sometimes so arranged as to suggest a grotesque human face, but this is the first example of an actual, carefully carved human face as the central motif of a surface decoration.

H.B.C.

165.
Weight for Throwing Board (Winged
    Object)
Okvik culture
St. Lawrence Island, Alaska
Ivory
7.7 cm (width)
78/472

165A

165B

165C

This human torso has the narrow, oval face, pointed head, and long thin nose that are the hallmarks of Okvik figurines, and the body itself is typically Okvik in form. The incised decoration on the body is something different. When I first described Okvik (Old Bering Sea style 1) art I called its linear decoration somewhat "scratchy" as compared with the graceful flowing lines of later Old Bering Sea art. On the present figurine the incised lines are scratchy indeed, with no attempt at organization or pattern.

H.B.C.

166.
Figurine
Okvik culture
St. Lawrence Island, Alaska
Ivory
19.1 cm (height)
78/451

This Okvik figurine is a combination of new and conventional features of the Okvik art style. The short stubby shoulders, long narrow nose, and treatment of the eyes are typically Okvik, but the head, instead of being pointed, is broad and rounded and the man seems to be wearing a hunting helmet. The lower end of the torso is rounded instead of flat. There is a carefully planned decoration of straight double lines, some spurred, on the body.

H.B.C.

167.
Figure Wearing Visor
Okvik culture
St. Lawrence Island, Alaska
Ivory
9.2 cm (height)
78/615

This fragmentary implement, which may belong to the Old Bering Sea culture, has been tentatively identified as a fat scraper. Such implements were used for the preliminary removal of fat from animal skins, the first step in the preparation of skins for clothing and other uses.

J.W.VS.

168.
Fat Scraper
Old Bering Sea culture
Bering Strait, Alaska
Ivory
17.0 cm (height)
78/616
See colour plate on page 31.

Cord attachers and drag handles made of walrus ivory were among the most imaginative of Eskimo art works. The carver made small sculptures, utilizing human, animal, and mythological shapes where a simple oval, round, or square piece of ivory would have served as well. These little objects, which were made for attaching additional lengths of cord to a line or to make loops (the larger ones were used as rope handles), perhaps doubled as charms or amulets during the hunt and its related activities.

Most of these objects – even comparatively simple ones like this animal head – were made with great care: eyes and nostrils were excavated for insets; and ears, mouths, and tongues were often realistically carved out. In this figurine, the mouth is closed, but the teeth are nevertheless marked on the outside by short perpendicular lines. A wolf mask was often characterized by the use of sharp wooden teeth, yet this ivory object looks more like a bear than a wolf.

Cord attachers and drag handles were made in seemingly endless variety by all Alaskan Eskimos, but their configurations generally fit into three categories: a complete animal or human body or animal or human face; a composite of one or more faces or bodies; and a composite in puzzle form, by which one part of a figure became part of another. The more simple attachers were usually, but not always, made in north Alaska, and the more complicated ones in southwest Alaska.

D.J.R.

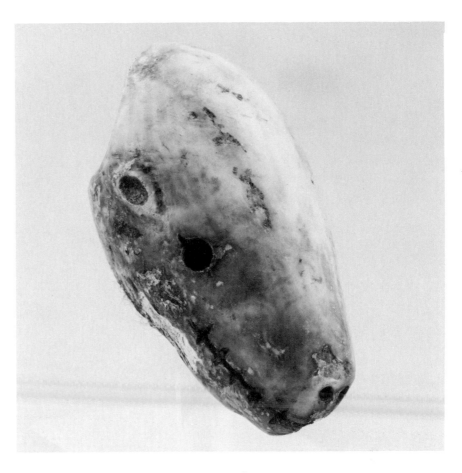

169.
Cord Attacher
Early nineteenth century
Northern Alaska (?)
Ivory
3.7 cm (height)
78/461

Pipes of walrus ivory tusk were prime souvenirs in the Bering Strait area of Alaska from the 1870s to the 1890s, when their popularity was superseded by whole tusks and cribbage boards engraved with pictorial subjects. Ivory pipes were made almost entirely as a vehicle for the creative prowess of the artist, usually manifested in a wealth of representational engravings, but sometimes in geometric designs or bas-relief sculpture of typical arctic subjects. Sometimes the realistic engravings and sculpture were combined, as in this pipe.

The souvenir pipes were apparently copied after the large wooden pipes that were introduced into Alaska from Siberia, along with tobacco, some time in the eighteenth century. The ivory pipes were made mainly at Saint Michael and in Seward Peninsula villages where a souvenir industry was fostered by trading companies, especially after the purchase of Alaska from Russia in 1867.

One of the unique aspects of early pipes such as this one is the almost exact transfer of pictographs – except for size, – from traditional objects to souvenirs. Furthermore, some of the traditional drill bows and souvenir pipes appear to have been engraved by the same man – early examples of Eskimo versatility with a hand dipped in two cultures simultaneously. The subject matter and engraving style of this pipe are similar to two drill bows collected in 1879 at Cape Nome (now in the Smithsonian Institution, USNM 44398 and 44399) and include walrus and whale hunting, villagers welcoming a visitor, pulling seals on the ice, camp scenes of dancing and fish drying, and an *umiak* stored on a rack. Unusual, however, is an engraving in a different style on the flat butt of the tusk at the bowl end, an area usually not engraved. In this case, it may have been done by another man or at a later time.

D.J.R.

170A

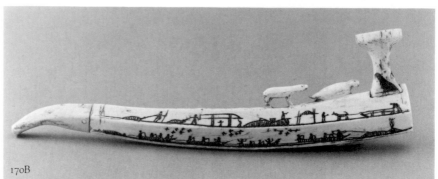

170B

170C

170.
Pipe with Pictorial Engravings
c. 1880
Cape Nome, Alaska (?)
Ivory and blacking
20.2 cm (length)
78/581

This roughly carved ivory amulet in the shape of a baleen whale may have been used in whaling ceremonies by the Eskimos of northwest Alaska. It could also have been kept with whaling gear in an *umiak* to bring good fortune when these great animals were being hunted. Similar amulets of stone, wood, and ivory from Sledge Island in Bering Strait and Point Barrow are described and illustrated by Nelson (*The Eskimo About Bering Strait*, p. 439, fig. 151) and Murdoch (*Ethnological Results of the Point Barrow Expedition*, pp. 403, 435, figs. 407, 421).

J.W.VS.

171.
Whaling Charm
Nineteenth century
Point Barrow or Point Hope, Alaska
Ivory
11.1 cm (length)
78/464

Although a ban on the sale of breech loading weapons and ammunition to the native peoples of Alaska was in effect until 1896, it was difficult to enforce and metallic cartridges were in use among the Eskimos of western Alaska after 1880. Since ammunition was never readily available, however, the reloading of spent cartridge cases was a necessity. This reloading tool consists of two pieces of ivory joined at the distal end by a metal rivet. One section has round holes to receive the cartridge cases. In the other section, opposite the holes, are (or were) tampers made from thick nails. Circle-dot decoration on Eskimo artifacts was common as early as the first millennium AD.

J.W.VS

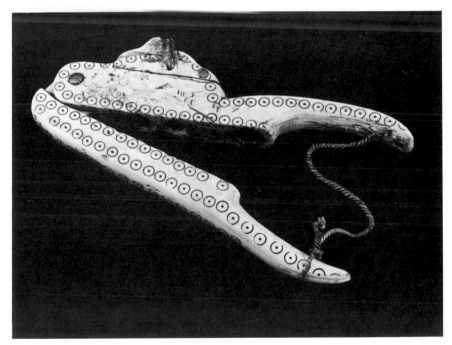

172.
Cartridge Reloader
Late nineteenth century
Seward Peninsula, Alaska (?)
Ivory, metal, hide, rope, and blacking
21.9 cm (length)
78/589

During historic times mythological and legendary creatures such as the one on this spoon – a caribou with flippers of a seal – were among the many pictorial subjects painted on wooden utensils by the southern, or Yupik-speaking, Eskimos of Alaska. The northern Eskimos, or Inupiat, also used graphic designs (in quite a different style), which they engraved on bone and ivory objects. The northerners rarely painted pictorial designs on wood, and the southerners rarely engraved them on ivory.

Probably more important than mythological subjects, at least by the end of the nineteenth century, was the portrayal of unusual events in a family's history. The story, which was usually painted in black outline with as few figures as possible, was executed for the first time on a bowl or a tray by a member of the family at the beginning of a festival, especially the messenger feast. Thereafter, the picture was always painted exactly the same. The story and design belonged to the family and could not be used by any other. Unlike the myriads of subjects and stories engraved on the northern ivory drill bows, a bowl or a spoon contained only one.

Most of the wooden utensils collected between 1877 and 1881 from the Kuskokwim River area by Edward William Nelson, the Smithsonian Institution collector, appear to have mythological subjects in much more imaginative and elaborate forms than those that have been made for sale since the 1930s by the Nunivak Islanders, the main suppliers of modern painted souvenir dishes and spoons. Of late, however, the Nunivak artists have concentrated on making wooden masks and sculpture with innovative designs rather than copying the traditional painted ware.

D.J.R.

173.
Spoon
Modern
Nunivak Island, Alaska
Wood and paint
22.9 cm (length)
78/450

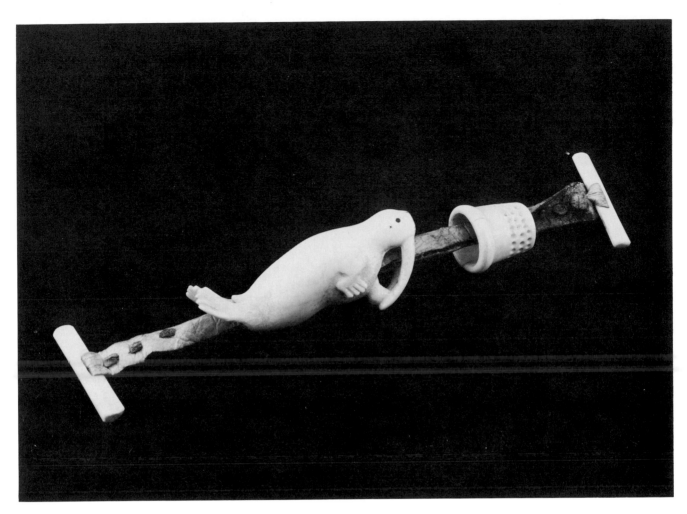

This needlecase is a modern version of an object that has been made by Eskimos for at least fifteen hundred years. Tubular needlecases from the Old Bering Sea period were decorated with geometric designs, but were rarely made in animal or human form. In the much later Thule period, the northern Eskimos from Point Barrow to Greenland made ivory needlecases with unique "wings," and in northwest Alaska, an unusual form was a human figure (usually a slender female) with a thong that passed from the top of the head through a hole in the feet. In precontact days a variety of small awls, needles, knives, sharpeners, and a thimble made of skin was attached to the thong.

During the nineteenth century, a popular needlecase was made in southwest Alaska from the hollow wingbone of a swan or a goose, lavishly ornamented with geometric designs, and stoppered on one end with a carved

wooden fish head, and at the other, with a carved wooden fish tail. The woman's sewing implements were placed inside the resulting container instead of on a thong.

This modern souvenir includes a copy in ivory of a non-Eskimo metal thimble and a walrus figurine, one of the all-time favourite subjects for market art, but not for traditional needlecases. In this example, the delicate tusks and flippers of the walrus would not have survived very long in a seamstress's sewing bag, or even attached to her belt, as was also the custom.

D.J.R.

174.
Needlecase
Modern
Alaska
Ivory, sealskin, baleen, and ink
18.4 cm (length)
78/465

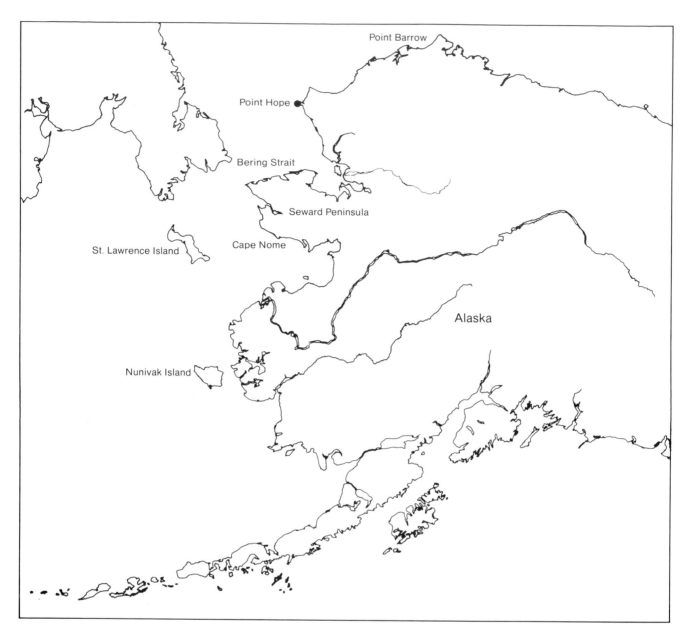

Point Barrow

Point Hope

Bering Strait

Seward Peninsula

Cape Nome

St. Lawrence Island

Nunivak Island

Alaska

MAP OF ALASKA

SELECTED BIBLIOGRAPHY

Agnes Etherington Art Centre
Inuit Art in the 1970's. Exhibition Catalogue. Kingston: Agnes Etherington Art Centre, 1979.

Art Gallery of Ontario
The People Within. Exhibition Catalogue. Toronto: Art Gallery of Ontario, 1976.

Barz, Sandra, editor
Inuit Artists Print Workbook. New York: Arts & Culture of the North, 1981.

Blodgett, Jean
The Coming and Going of the Shaman: Eskimo Shamanism and Art. Exhibition Catalogue. Winnipeg: The Winnipeg Art Gallery, 1979.

"The Historic Period in Canadian Eskimo Art." *The Beaver* (Summer 1979), pp. 17-27.

Karoo Ashevak. Exhibition Catalogue. Winnipeg: The Winnipeg Art Gallery, 1977.

Kenojuak. Toronto: Mintmark Press, 1981.

Looking South. Exhibition Catalogue. Winnipeg: The Winnipeg Art Gallery, 1978.

Tuu'luq/Anguhadluq. Exhibition Catalogue. Winnipeg: The Winnipeg Art Gallery, 1976.

Butler, Sheila
"Wall Hangings from Baker Lake." *The Beaver* (Autumn 1972), pp. 26-31.

Canadian Eskimo Arts Council
Crafts from Arctic Canada. Exhibition Catalogue. Ottawa: Canadian Eskimo Arts Council, 1974.

Sculpture. Exhibition Catalogue. Ottawa: Canadian Eskimo Arts Council, 1970.

Sculpture/Inuit: Masterworks of the Canadian Arctic. Exhibition Catalogue. Toronto: University of Toronto Press, 1971.

Collins, Henry B.
Archaeology of St. Lawrence Island, Alaska. Smithsonian Miscellaneous Collection, vol. XCVI, no. 1 (1937), pp. 1-431.

"Eskimo Art." *The Far North: 2000 Years of American Eskimo and Indian Art.* Exhibition Catalogue. Washington, DC: National Gallery of Art, 1973.

"Eskimo Cultures." *Encyclopedia of World Art*, vol. V, cols. 1-28. New York: McGraw-Hill Book Company, Inc., 1961.

Department of Indian Affairs and Northern Development, Canada
Inuit Artists Biography Files. Inuit Art Section, Ottawa.

Driscoll, Bernadette
The Inuit Amautik: I Like My Hood to Be Full. Exhibition Catalogue. Winnipeg: The Winnipeg Art Gallery, 1980.

Inuit Myths, Legends and Songs. Exhibition Catalogue. Winnipeg: The Winnipeg Art Gallery, 1982.

Eber, Dorothy, editor
Pitseolak: Pictures Out of My Life. Montreal: Design Collaborative Books in association with Oxford University Press, Toronto, 1971.

Fitzhugh, Willian W., Susan A. Kaplan et al
Inua: Spirit World of the Bering Sea Eskimo. Exhibition Catalogue. Washington, DC: Smithsonian Institution Press for the National Museum of Natural History, 1982.

Gallery One-One-One
Tiktak. Exhibition Catalogue. Winnipeg: The University of Manitoba Press, 1970.

Kritzwiser, Kay
"Tookoome, the hunter, is also an artist." *Globe and Mail* (Toronto), 9 July, 1976.

Houston, James
Eskimo Prints. Barre, Massachusetts: Barre Publishers, 1967.

Lamour, W. T.
Keewatin Eskimo Ceramics '67. Ottawa: The Department of Indian Affairs and Northern Development, 1967.

Murdoch, John
Ethnological Results of the Point Barrow Expedition. U.S. Bureau of Ethnology, Ninth Annual Report. Washington, DC: US Government Printing Office, 1892.

Myers, Marybelle, editor
Davidialuk. Montreal: La Fédération des Coopératives du Nouveau-Québec, 1977.

Joe Talirunili. Montreal: La Fédération des Coopératives du Nouveau-Québec, 1977.

Things Made by Inuit. Exhibition Catalogue. Montreal: La Fédération des Coopératives du Nouveau-Québec, 1980.

Nagy, Hendrika
"Pottery in Keewatin." *The Beaver* (Autumn 1967), pp. 61-66.

The National Gallery of Canada
Cape Dorset: A Decade of Eskimo Prints and Recent Sculpture. Exhibition Catalogue. Ottawa: The National Gallery of Canada, 1967.

National Museum of Man
The Inuit Print. Exhibition Catalogue. Ottawa: National Museum of Man, National Museums of Canada, 1977.

Nelson, Edward W.
The Eskimo About Bering Strait. Bureau of American Ethnology, Eighteenth Annual Report. Washington, DC: Smithsonian Institution, 1899.

Norman Mackenzie Art Gallery
The Jacqui and Morris Shumiatcher Collection of Inuit Art. Exhibition Catalogue. Regina: Norman Mackenzie Art Gallery, 1981.

Raine, David F.
"The Miniatures of Bobby Takrik." *The Beaver* (Winter 1971), pp. 16-17.

Rasmussen, Knud
Intellectual Culture of the Iglulik Eskimos. Report of the Fifth Thule Expedition 1921-24, vol. VII, no. 1. Copenhagen: Gyldendalske Boghandel, Nordisk Forlag, 1929.

Ray, Dorothy Jean
Aleut and Eskimo Art: Tradition and Innovation in South Alaska. Seattle: University of Washington Press, 1981.

Eskimo Art: Tradition and Innovation in North Alaska. Seattle: University of Washington Press, 1977.

Roberts, A. Barry
The Inuit Artists of Inoucdjouac, P.Q. Montreal: La Fédération des Coopératives du Nouveau-Québec with the cooperation of the Department of Indian and Northern Affairs, 1978.

The Inuit Artists of Sugluk, P.Q. Montreal: La Fédération des Coopératives du Nouveau-Québec with the cooperation of the Department of Indian and Northern Affairs, 1976.

Roch, Ernst, editor
  Arts of the Eskimo: Prints. Montreal: Signum Press, 1974.

Ryan, Terrence
  "Drawings from the People." *North,* vol. XI, no. 5 (September-October 1964), pp. 25-31.

Saladin d'Anglure, Bernard et al
  La parole changée en pierre. Vie et oeuvre de Davidialuk Alasuaq, artiste inuit du Québec arctique. Gouvernement du Québec, Ministère des Affaires culturelles, Direction génerale du patrimonine, numéro 11 dans la série les cahiers du Patrimonie. Québec: l'Imprimerie Laflamme, 1978.

Surrey Art Gallery
  Sculpture of the Inuit. Exhibition Catalogue. Surrey: Surrey Art Gallery, 1978.

Swinton, George
  Eskimo Sculpture. Toronto: McClelland and Stewart, 1965.

  Sculpture of the Eskimo. Toronto: McClelland and Stewart, 1972.

Swinton, Nelda
  The Inuit Sea Goddess. Exhibition Catalogue. Montreal: The Montreal Museum of Fine Arts, 1980.

Van de Velde, Father Franz, O.M.I.
  Canadian Eskimo Artists: A Biographical Dictionary: Pelly Bay. Yellowknife: Government of the Northwest Territories, 1970.

Watt, Virginia J., editor
  Canadian Guild of Crafts Quebec: The Permanent Collection. Montreal: Canadian Guild of Crafts Quebec, 1980.

West Baffin Eskimo Cooperative
  Kiawak Ashoona: Sculpture. Exhibition Catalogue. Cape Dorset: Kingait Press, 1980.

  Parr: A Print Retrospective. Exhibition Catalogue. Cape Dorset: Kingait Press, 1979.

  Pitseolak. Exhibition Catalogue. Cape Dorset: West Baffin Eskimo Cooperative in cooperation with the Department of Indian and Northern Affairs, 1975.

The Winnipeg Art Gallery
  Baker Lake Drawings. Exhibition Catalogue. Winnipeg: The Winnipeg Art Gallery, 1972.

  The Bessie Bulman Collection. Exhibition Catalogue. Winnipeg: The Winnipeg Art Gallery, 1973

  Cape Dorset. Exhibition Catalogue. Winnipeg: The Winnipeg Art Gallery, 1979.

  Eskimo Carvers of Keewatin NWT. Exhibition Catalogue. Winnipeg: The Winnipeg Art Gallery, 1964.

  Eskimo Sculpture. Exhibition Catalogue. Winnipeg: The Winnipeg Art Gallery, 1967.

  Port Harrison/Inoucdjouac. Exhibition Catalogue. Winnipeg: The Winnipeg Art Gallery, 1977.

  Povungnituk. Exhibition Catalogue. Winnipeg: The Winnipeg Art Gallery, 1977.

  Rankin Inlet. Exhibition Catalogue. Winnipeg: The Winnipeg Art Gallery, 1980.

  Repulse Bay. Exhibition Catalogue. Winnipeg: The Winnipeg Art Gallery, 1978.

  The Zazelenchuk Collection of Eskimo Art. Exhibition Catalogue. Winnipeg: The Winnipeg Art Gallery, 1978.

Zazelenchuk, Stanley
  "Kavik: The Man and the Artist." *Arts & Culture of the North,* vol. IV, no. 2 (Spring 1980), pp. 219-221.

Baker Lake print catalogues:

1970, 1971, 1972, 1973, 1974, 1975, 1976, 1977, 1978, 1979, 1980, 1981, 1982

Cape Dorset print catalogues:

1959, 1960, 1961, 1962, 1963, 1964-65, 1966, 1967, 1968, 1969, 1970, 1971, 1972, 1973, 1974, 1975, 1976, 1977, 1978, 1979, 1980, 1981

Povungnituk print catalogues:

1962, 1964, 1965, 1966, 1968, 1969, 1960-70, 1972, 1973, 1975, 1976, 1977, 1978, 1980

GLOSSARY

amaut	carrying pouch on back of woman's parka
amautik	woman's parka
angakoq	shaman
atteegee	inner parka
Inuit	the people (plural of Inuk)
Inuk	person, human
inukshuk	cairn built of rocks, may be in shape of human figure
Inuktitut	the Inuit language
kamik	skin boot
kamotik	sled
kudlik	traditional oil lamp
ulu	woman's knife
umiak	sealskin boat

INDEX

PHOTO CREDITS

All photographs are by Larry Ostrom, Photographic Services, Art Gallery of Ontario, with the following exceptions:

J. A. Chambers Nos. 164-174 (black and white only); Department of Indian Affairs and Northern Development, Ottawa figs. 6, 9, 11; Ernest Mayer figs. 1-5, 10, 22, 25, 27-28; Michael Mitchell figs. 20, 26; National Museum of Man, National Museums of Canada, Ottawa figs. 12, 13, 21, 23; Tom Prescott figs. 8, 17; Public Archives Canada fig. 19; University Museum of Archaeology and Ethnology, Cambridge fig. 24.

DOCUMENTARY PHOTOGRAPHY

p. 33, Baker Lake: top: by Michael Neill, 1980; bottom: Craft Center, by K. J. Butler, Sanavik Cooperative, 1971. p. 70, Cape Dorset: upper left by Jean Blodgett, 1980; lower left: Printshop, left to right, Ottochie, Lukta, Saggiaktok, Eegyvudluk, Ningoochiak, Terrence Ryan, Pee, Liasa by George Hunter, 1978; right: Ottochie by Tessa Macintosh, 1975. p. 147, Clyde River: by Gabriel Gély, 1980. p. 150, Eskimo Point: by Jean Blodgett, 1972. p. 62, Frobisher Bay: by Jimmy Manning, 1982. p. 166, Great Whale River by Odette Leroux, National Museum of Man, National Museums of Canada, 1982. p. 170, Inukjuak: by Jean Blodgett, 1980. p. 183, Lake Harbour: upper: by Charles Gimpel, 1958; lower: by Gary Milligan, 1980. p. 188, Pelly Bay: by Gabriel Gély, 1966. p. 200, Povungnituk: top: by Jean Blodgett, 1980; bottom: Kanayook by Odette Leroux, National Museum of Man, National Museums of Canada, 1982. p. 212, Ranklin Inlet: upper: by Bruce Myers, 1965; lower: by Jean Blodgett, 1972. p. 225, Repulse Bay: by Gabriel Gély, 1982. p. 238, Spence Bay: Karoo Ashevak by Pamela Harris, 1972. p. 242, Sugluk: by Leslie Boyd, 1980. p. 249, Unknown: by Odette Leroux, National Museum of Man, National Museums of Canada, 1982. p. 252, Artifacts (Alaska): Gambell, St. Lawrence Island by Gabriel Gély, 1972.

Contemporary Canadian Inuit works of art reproduced by permission of the following Cooperatives on behalf of the artists:

La Fédération des Coopératives du Nouveau-Québec, Montreal (on behalf of Great Whale River, Inukjuak, Povungnituk and Sugluk, Arctic Quebec); Igutaq Group, Clyde River, NWT; Ikaluit Cooperative, Frobisher Bay, NWT; Kimik Cooperative, Lake Harbour, NWT; Kissarvik Cooperative, Rankin Inlet, NWT; Koomiut Cooperative, Pelly Bay, NWT; Naujat Cooperative, Repulse Bay, NWT; Padlei Cooperative, Eskimo Point, NWT; West Baffin Eskimo Cooperative, Cape Dorset, NWT.

Karoo Ashevak sculptures reproduced with the permission of the Public Trustee Officer, Department of Justice and Public Service, Government of the Northwest Territories.

Composition: Canadian Composition Limited
Separations: Graphic Litho-Plate Inc.
Lithography: The Bryant Press Limited
Binding: The Bryant Press Limited
Film: Black and White: Rodney-Spencer Graphics Inc.
Colour: Graphic Litho-Plate Inc.
Set in Magna Carta and printed on 80 lb Patina Coated Matte